Spiritual Gifts

An analysis of the biblical evidence concerning the discovery of the practical motivational power of the Holy Spirit in the life of believers and the manifestations of His work in the local churches

Don Fanning

First Edition 2011

Spiritual Gifts
by Don Fanning

Cover, by page design by Krista Freeman

Published by
Branches Publications
1985 Colby Dr.
Forest, Virginia 24551

Copyright © 2011: Branches Publications
        Don Fanning

ISBN 978-0-9833290-7-7

Preface

The Lord never asks us to do things that He does not equip us to accomplish. The power of the Holy Spirit indwelling every believer has so many benefits and enabling capabilities that it would be impossible without Him to even begin to fulfill our ministry and impact in the world's cultures.

Our message in the proclamation of the gospel is empowered by the Spirit to bring conviction, illumination and drawing of the listening sinner, while giving the speaker the giftedness to clearly and persuasively announce with boldness the message of salvation to the unsaved of the world.

This dual empowerment of the Spirit within the believer enables the performance of service and ministry for others through the spiritual gifts and the working of the Spirit in the lives of the recipients of this service, which results in the ebb and flow of loving relationships and Christ-like character transformation.

This study will focus on the biblical evidence regarding the spiritual gifts with some reasonable conjectures and deductions to help identify manifestations of the different gifted areas of the church's ministries.

The manifestations of the spiritual gifts has enormous variations with general similarities. The Spirit sovereignly decides which gifts are delegated to every believer at the moment He begins indwelling each new believer (1 Cor 12:4, 7, 11).

The Lord Jesus decides the specific type of gifted ministry that each spiritual gift will empower (1 Cor 12:5). Following His leadership in one's life will lead the believer into their special kind of ministry of every specific gift.

Finally, the Father determines the result or extent of the ministry of each of the gifts that every believer has received (1 Cor 12:6). The entire Trinity is involved in the ministry potential of every believer. To remain ignorant or indifferent to this vast divine enabling of believers is to dishonor the purpose of God in bringing us to Himself. For these reasons Paul wrote various passages to instruct the churches of the ages how God enables the believers to have the power of God in fulfilling their divine purpose in this life.

It is the prayer of this author that the reader will resonate with one or more of the descriptions in this manual, sensing a personal identity with one or more spiritual gifts, then with confidence begin to pray and dream about how God will use His empowerment in your life for service to benefit hundreds or thousands of others to the honor and glory of our Savior. The privilege of serving our Lord is made practical and effective by how we lovingly care for His people, His church, His body, and His honor. The Spirit's power enables every believer to be effective and self-sacrificing as they live for others in the model of our Savior's life. This is the purpose of the spiritual gifts.

Contents

Introduction:

The nature of the church calls for its members to recognize their respective capabilities and to begin functioning in the areas of their particular ministries. Just as the physical body is one organism having many parts: arms, legs, hands, feet, etc., each one with their respective functions, which operate in different manners, but at the same time in harmony and unity, so is the Body of Christ, the Church; unity in the midst of diversity.

If the body is going to function as an organism, then it is necessary for the members to minister or serve one another with all the capabilities that the Holy Spirit has given to each one. Each local church, that is the Body functioning in miniature, requires spiritual maturity, biblical understanding and the recognition (and use) of the gifts of each member.

This study of the spiritual gifts given to the churches is (1) a study of the passages that describe the gifts of the Spirit, and (2) a description of the gifts.

The power of the Spirit flows in the church through the expression of the God given gifts. The gift is not in itself the purpose or goal for the believer, rather it is simply the means through which the Spirit can minister to others through that member. The possession of a gift in itself does not measure spirituality. The gift functions as a canal or funnel. It is not the product, but the means of delivery of the product. The Spirit utilizes these gifts to edify individuals in the church, in order to facilitate the transformation of others into the image of Christ and to motivate the extension of the church in the world.

In spite of the importance of recognizing and practicing one's gifts, it is not necessary to be frustrated in your search; that is, the priority should be one's spiritual maturity, knowledge of the Scriptures with it's wisdom and assurances, and the service for the Lord that He designed for every life. If you sense a need in your church, which is not being satisfied, perhaps you should try to meet that need. If there are few or no conversions and you know an unbeliever, do whatever possible to bring them to a knowledge of Christ. Occupy yourself in serving the Lord by meeting the needs you perceive, and your gifts will quickly become obvious. Experience shows that there are times when the Lord delays in making evident our gifts in order that we grow sufficiently mature and committed to using them faithfully in His service and through His power. The important thing is that we learn to minister and serve one another.

When you finish this study on the gifts you will be able...

1.   To write a list of the gifts of the New Testament, locate them in the NT and define them in your own words.
2.   To identify at least one spiritual gift, which God has given to you.
3.   To know how to help others discover and define their spiritual gifts and ministry.
4.   To contribute to the ministry of the church through your gifted ministry and motivate others to discover their own ministries.

Note: We should not be ignorant concerning the spiritual gifts (1 Cor 12:1, "Now concerning spiritual gifts, brethren, I do not want you to be ignorant."

Some clarifications in the study of the gifts

Introduction: The two extremes that have negative consequences.
1. Avoid or intentionally ignore a subject (usually because there are disagreements)
2. Overemphasize the gifts to the extreme that the development of the spiritual life and the transformation to the similitude of Christ, in His character, become secondary goals.

Problems:
1. There are disagreements between different Bible believers concerning the definition of the gifts and the actual validity of some of the gifts.
2. There is considerable ignorance and carelessness about the spiritual gifts in many churches, perhaps because of fear of divisiveness or indefensible positions.
3. There is considerable confusion regarding the relationship between the spiritual gifts and the natural abilities or talents of the believer.
4. Certain gifts are emphasized by some believers as if they were indispensable evidences of a spiritual character. Unfortunately in some cases such an emphasis generates an unhealthy pride, and in the worst case, divisions.

Principles for confronting the problems:
a. The disagreements between Bible believing churches normally indicate a lack of clear Biblical evidence in order to resolve the issue. Thus there should be a certain tolerance shown toward expressing different opinions that do not violate the clear directives of the Scriptures.
b. When you begin to emphasize the gifts, do it slowly. Look for the gifts in your personal life. Every time it is possible, recognize the gifts that have been used in your church. Look for what is most evident in your life and surrounding ministry.
c. Do not worry about distinguishing between gifts and talents. Use both in the service of the Lord. Trust that God will show the necessary distinctions.
d. Be careful not to emphasize some spiritual gifts to the exclusion of others. Distinguish between the exercise of the gift in the church (which should be actively motivated) and the use of a gift as a sign of spirituality (which should be denied). There is a significant difference between the fruit of the Spirit and the gifts of the Spirit. The fruit of the Spirit indicates spiritual maturity and the gifts indicate the motivation for serving others.

Distinction between the gifts and the fruit of the Spirit:

Gifts of the Spirit	Fruit of the Spirit
1. Different for every believer	1. Same for every believer, without exception.
2. related to the ministry to others	2. Related to our inner character.
3. Classified according to importance and necessary emphasis in the church ministries.	3. No classification as all the aspects of the fruit of the Spirit are essential and equally important
4. Can be abused, cause offenses and divisions.	4. Never can be used badly if authentic.
5. No Christian has all the gifts.	5. All believer should manifest all the fruit
6. No single gift is obligated for all believers.	6. All aspects of the fruit are commanded to be manifested in the believer's life.

Conclusions:
1. The ideal in the Christian life is to join the exercise of the gifts of the Spirit with the expression of the fruit of the Spirit (all 9 aspects) simultaneously.
2. Both the fruit and the gifts of the Spirit are signs of the presence of the Spirit
3. Maturity is manifested, through the likeness of Christ and the manifestation of the fruit of the Spirit. The presence of the gifts does not guarantee a likeness to Christ in our lives.

Steps to discover and develop your spiritual gift(s)

Section I. Study the passages that describe the gifts
1.   Make a list of all the gifts in each of the four passages that describe the gifts.
2.   Look for principles that govern the gifts.

Section II. Study the application of the gifts until you can recognize the activities in other believers

1.   Make a personal biblical study of the gifts.
2.   Look for biblical illustrations of gifted personas. Make a list of what you can find in the Bible.
3.   Study the lives of Christian leaders that are identified with your gifts. Make another list.
4.   Identify the gifts manifested in the lives of believers that you know.

Section III. Analyze yourself and identify which are your spiritual gifts
1.   Use the survey over your personal convictions.
2.   Remember that if you walk in the Spirit (not in the flesh), your desires will come from God.
3.   Ask other Christians who understand the significance of the gifts to confirm which are your spiritual gifts.
4.   Ask someone with the gift of wisdom, discernment, teaching or exhortation to give you some additional suggestions regarding your gifts.
5.   Ask some intimate friends to comment on their ideas of which are your gifts.
6.   Principally ask the leaders of your church for their observations.

Section IV. Let your experience be a determining factor in the manifestation of your gifts.
1.   Your church will be more and more conscience of your gifts as you work in its programs.
2.   You will be conscious of the fruit that results from the exercise of your gift in the lives of others.
3.   You will feel a conscious satisfaction in what you are doing.
4.   You will recognize that those with gifts, especially the gift of leadership, are going to attract others with similar gifts.
5.   Complete the survey of your personal experiences.

Section V. The gifts that have been chosen must be put into practice. Begin with the suggested plan of development of your gifts. Choose a ministry area in the sphere of your gifts and commit yourself to use them from now on.
1.   Follow the procedures that are recommended according to the gifts chosen.
2.   Write in your own words a plan for how you will seek to develop your gifts.
3.   Write the area or type of service that you will seek to fulfill in the future.
4.   Write the desire of your heart about what you want to complete for the Lord with your gifts or ministries.

Section I

Principles, analysis and location of the gifts of the Spirit

I. Principles of the gifts from Romans 12:1-8

A. The following are a series of principles, concepts or directives derived from the key verses in our pssage. You can verify the statements, or tweak them for your understanding of the gifts. This is where we receive our guidance for understanding and practice of all of the gifts.
1. Everyone of us should evaluate ourselves in terms of our gifts (12:3).
2. We should recognize that our gifts are different from others and thus we have liberty to follow our hearts as we use them, and not be forced into imitating the service of someone else (12:6).
3. We should exercise our gifts according to our faith (our understanding of the will of God) given by the guidance of God (12:6).
4. The motive for the use of our gifts and the attitude about their use, are as important as the actual exercise of the gifts ("according to the measure of faith", "with liberality", "with joy" (12:8).
5. Each one should have the opportunity to use his gifts in a team structure (12:4-6).

B. Explanation of the gifts mentioned in Rom 12

Gifts Mentioned	Purpose of the Gift	Genuine manifestaion
Prophecy	The receipt and proclamation of divine, infalible revelation.	Proclamation of revealed truth with power and conviction, which always comes to pass.
Service, helps or ministry	Meets material needs of others.	Material service supplied with great sacrifice under the direction and wisdom of the Spirit.
Teaching	Illumination of the understanding of the revelation given by the apostles and prophets in the Word.	Clear communication of the principles, meanings of words in context, and grammar of the text (Eph 1:16-19).
Exhortation	Maintain the purity and obedience to the Word.	Advice, consolation, counseling, motivating to obedience to the Word.
Giving	Economic and materila support for the ministry and needy people.	Sharing of personal possessions freely under the guidance of the Spirit.
Administration, leadership	Maintain the order, direction and motivation for the church.	Acts of love inspired by the Spirit to the unloved and rejected.
Mercy	Demonstrate a compassion heart for the undeserving and needy.	Caring for the unlovely and needy through acts of sacrifice.

II.   Principles in 1 Corinthians 12-14

A. The following are a series of principles, concepts or directives derived from the key verses in our pssage. This is where we receive our guidance for understanding and practice of all of the gifts.

12:1 Ignorance of the gifts can produce abuses.
12:2 Unusual or phenominal experiences do not necessarily indicate the work of the Spirit.
12:3 A proof of the activity of the Spirit is that there is always an exaltation of the deity of Christ.
12:4 The Spirit produces DIVERSITY of the gifts, not SIMILARITY.
12:5 Christ motivates a variety manifestations of SERVICES (*diaconia*) of the gifts for the benefit of others.
12:6 The Father provides the variety of EFFECTS (*energematon*, "power") or results.
12:7 The MANIFESTATION of at least one ability of the Spirit is given to every believer.
12:7 The PURPOSE is for the benefit of everyone else. It is not for one's self.

12:11 The gifts are not given on the basis of merit, or as a result of desire, requests, or spirituality, rather by a sovereign decision of the Spirit.

12:12 Unity results from the diversity of the gifts. Divisiveness is evidence of the flesh, due to exaggerated emphasis of one gift over others.

12:13 The Body of Christ is formed by the Baptism of the Spirit, which puts the believer into a union, inseparable with Christ at the moment the Spirit enters his life. Power comes from being united to Christ.

12:14 A body requires distinct members (i.e., gifts in this context) to function.

12:15 No member (gift) is inferior (or superior) to any other. The body depends on and needs all of the gifts.

12:16 To desire the special attention given to some of the members (gifts) is egotism.

12:17 No one member is equal to or as important as the whole body, although some may be more recognized.

12:18 God Himself created our abilities. It is not our election that determines our gifts.

12:19 To insist that one gift is universal is to create a monster, i.e., like a body being made of just an ear.

12:21 The more visible gifts need the less visible ones. Their importance should not be overemphasized.

12:22 People with "weak" gifts are more sensitive to being wounded; they require protection and recognition.

12:24 The more recognized gifts do not need more recognition, rather God's way of blending together the body is to give more honor to the lesser gifts. His plan is to create equality.

12:25 Egotism and envy cause division. Our focus should be in serving others in harmony.

12:26 If one gift suffers, they all suffer; if one gift is recognized, all should rejoice together.

12:27 Each member of the body is only a part of the total, but the contribution of each is essential.

12:31 There should be great care that the gifts in the highest category are prioritized in function.

13:1-3 Any gift or ability that is not motivated by love to others (i.e. selfishly) is useless and vain.

13:4 Love motivates the gifts to be patient, always beneficial to others, not seeking fame or recognition, never exaggerates its own importance to others, nor is prideful.

13:5 Love motivates the gifts to never embarrass another, to never be selfish, nor easily offended nor remembers hurts or offenses.

13:6 Love motivates the gifts to have no delight in divisions or injustices, but to be glad when the Word is understood and applied in lives.

13:7 Love motivates the gifts to overlook the faults of others, to accept their word, to see the best in others and to never be discouraged in the service of others even if not appreciated.

13:8 Love motivates the gifts to be constant, although some gifts were not designed to be permanent: prophecy, tongues and knowledge were to be terminated in a short time period.

13:9 Love motivated service is superior because knowledge and prophecy have only a temporary, one-time, limited or partial function.

13:10 The time of termination of these three temporary gifts is when their "perfection," "completion" or "fulfillment" comes, (the meanings of "perfect"), that is, when all the "parts" of their revelation are complete.

13:11 The reason for setting aside these three gifts is the relative maturity stage of the church, that is, they have revealed all the knowledge of God's will. Their function is complete.

13:12 Before the completion of the revelation of all God's Word even Paul did not understand all of the will of God as is now possible to those who have the completed revelation.

13:13 For the duration of the church age the chief motivations are to be confidence in the revealed Word, assurance that the promises will be fulfilled and the eternal motivation of love

14:1 The "best" gifts of the five categories in 12:28, should be prioritized. The maximum gift in the time of revelation (Paul's lifetime) was prophecy, but when its function was fulfilled the next priority on the listing became teaching for exhortation.

14:2 Paul made a difference between the "tongue" and "tongues". The former was ecstatic and emotional, while the plural was the genuine gift. Here the gift is singular, making reference to the pagan practice that had infiltrated the church, in which the "spirit" of man pretended to speak "mysteries" such as the pagan sects proclaimed. This was a false tongue without benefit to anyone in the church.

14:3 The genuine gift is for the benefit of others, producing in them edification or "strengthening", exhortation and consolation that comes from the translation of the message.

14:4 The false gift (singular) has a selfish motivation, building up of one's self or ego, which is contrasted with the genuine gift of prophecy, which builds up the whole church and maturing of individual.

14:5 The genuine gift (plural) could be beneficial, in contrast to the false gift, but always will be inferior to prophecy. If the tongues are interpreted, the interpretation could result in strengthening the whole church (as prophecy does), but without interpretation it is useless, even if genuine. Thus this gift can never stand alone.

14:6 In the time of Paul, the Word of God was not fully written (1 Corinthians was the 3rd book of the NT written), thus the church was dependent upon continual revelation for preaching and teaching. Speaking in tongues alone would not result in a revelation, prophecy, knowledge or teaching, thus was useless.

14:7-9 The false tongue (singular) is compared to noises made with musical instruments without musical composition. Absolutely nothing is communicated, nor people blessed. A tongue has to be understood to be genuine.

14:10 The genuine tongues (plural) are actual "idioms" in the world. A genuine tongue must have "meaning", that is distinguishing sounds for grammar and phonetics.

14:12-13 The emphasis and priority to function in love is to make sure all the gifts edify others. If it is not possible to interpret the tongue (singular), then the speaker remain silent, and pray that a gifted interpreter give an interpretation, which could edify the church.

14:14-15 Paul gives the illustration that if he were to pray in a tongue (singular) neither he nor anyone else would benefit. Paul determined that he would always pray with his mind and sing with his mind fully understanding what he was saying. Thus Paul never prayed or sang in an ecstatic tongue (singular). If he spoke in a tongue it was a language others understood.

14:16-17 When they prayed in the early church, only one prayed at a time, while others understanding and agreeing with the prayer would say "Amen!" When someone supposedly is speaking in his "spirit" no one can join him in prayer, nor be encouraged by such a prayer.

14:18-22 Paul spoke in tongues (plural) frequently, but never in the church. It was a sign to the Jews (Isa 26:11-12), who were expecting such a sign to confirm the new revelation.

14:23 The gift of tongues (plural) before the unconverted Gentiles made no sense, was crazy. It was useless for evangelism of gentiles.

14:24-25 Prophecy, on the other hand, would produce genuine conviction with the result of a profound conversion, when prophecy completed its function of delivering the completed Word of God, the the Word would have the same impact as the Early Church prophet.

14:26 Anything spoken in the congregation should have the purpose of edifying or building up the believers with wisdom and knowledge that can be understood and acted upon.

14:27 If anyone should want to speak in a tongue (singular) they are limited to two or three per meeting, taking turns and only if someone present can immediately interpret the words spoken.

14:28 If there is no interpreter present, then it is prohibited that anyone speak in such a tongue. The fruit of the Spirit is "…self-control" (Gal 5:23), thus a Spirit-filled person has control of himself always.

14:29 The same rule applies to the prophecies that were being revealed to the early church, only two or three in any given congregational meeting could speak, and that by turns. The rest of the congregation had the responsibility to "judge or evaluate" what was said, to determine if it were true or false (1 Jn 4:1).

14:30 Even if someone received a revelation while someone else was speaking, he would remain quiet and never interrupt the service of another. The Spirit-filled person has control of himself.

14:31 The love purpose of the speaking gifts are biblical understanding and encouragement.

14:32 The true gift of the Spirit always is controllable, because the fruit of the Spirit produces "self-control" (Gal 5:23). If someone looses control of himself, he is not under the power of the Spirit of God.

14:33 Disorder is the result of several people speaking different things simultaneously, which creates confusion. God does not have control of the meeting.

14:34-36 Another symptom that God is not in control is when women assume the teaching and leadership roles in the congregation. Paul would later reveal that women should never teach men nor assume authority over men in the congregation (1 Tim 2:9-15).

14:37 Paul did not write recommendations or mere opinions. He was an apostle. He wrote the commands of our Lord. No one is to be considered spiritual who does not take his written words seriously and finally.

14:39 The priority is communicating the biblical revelation in teaching and exhortation (14:31), but if someone has the gift of tongues (plural, that is an actual dialect), do not prohibit him from speaking as long as he complies with the previous requirements.

14:40 The evidence of the power and presence of God in a congregational meeting is when everything is done "decently" (respect is shown) and in order ("of quality and succession").

B. The gifts mentioned in 1 Corinthians 12-14

Gifts	Purpose	Genuine Manifestation
Apostle	Be the representative of Jesus in the foundation of the church and the source of divine revelaition	Someone personally elected personally by Jesus to be a witness of His earthly ministry and resurrection (Acts 1:21-22) and empowered to confirm Jesus' message with miraculous signs (2 Cor 12:12).
Prophecy	See Romans 12 description	
Teaching	See Romans 12 description	
Word of Knowledge	Enabled to declare the revelation of God given to this person by special revelation.	Receive in the mind new revelation that God was making known to the church. To understand, organize and communicate the thinking of God. It would be impossible to discover such concepts by human reason or intuition.
Word of Wisdom	Enabled to see the practical application of the principles and commands of the Word of God to life's situations.	Clarity and perception of how to apply the Word to individual lives so that they are transformed.
Faith	Enabled to perceive what God wants to do in present time and trust His involvement.	Faith given by the Spirit to trust in the intervention of God to show His power.
Miracles	Enabled to perform special miraculous signs to confirm the message of revelation.	Intervention of the power of God to prove His power is greater than that of Satan.
Healing	Enable to perform evident and incontrovertable and instantaneous miraculous healing.	A special authority given by Jesus for special signs and demonstration of His divine power.
Discerning spirits	Enable to discern the credibility of itenerate teachers protecting the church from false teachers and seducing spirits.	A capacity to distinguish betweenthe Spirit, flesh and other spirit-influences behind messages.
Tongues	Enabled to speak in foreign languages, especiall as a sign to Israel.	Miraculous ability to speak recognizable languages spoken miraculously for a sign to unbelievers.
Interpretation of tongues	Enable to interpret foreign languages spoken whether from the gift of tongues or a foreigner.	Miraculous interpretation of a language spoken in the church.
Helps	See Romans 12 description	
Administration	See Romans 12 description	

III. Principles of Ephesians 4:7-16

A. The following are a series of principles, concepts or directives derived from the key verses in our pssage. You can verify the statements, or tweak them for your understanding of the gifts. This is where we receive our guidance for understanding and practice of all of the gifts.

4:7 To every believer there has been given "grace" (*charis*, not the charismata, "gifts" in 1 Cor. 12) so that the gifts (discussed in 4:8-16) will function for the glory of God. This grace is the capacity to serve one another in love and humility (4:2-3), which results in unity. This grace is given in different measures to each believer and also the faith to exercise each ministry (Rom 12:3). This implies an enormous variety of manifestations of the gifts.

4:8 According to the prophecy from Psa 68:18, upon arrival in heaven after the ascension, Jesus began to give "gifts" (*domata*) to men in the churches as a triumphant Conqueror. This is part of His "booty," which was won at the cross.

4:11 Jesus Himself gave certain gifted men to the church. He gave men as apostles and prophets for the foundation of the church (2:20). He also gave gifted men as evangelists, pastors and teachers to continue the development and establishment of the church.

4:12 The principle responsibility of gifted evangelists-pastors-teachers is to continue the work of the gifted apostles-prophets by "equipping" or "making complete" (see Heb 13:20-21) all church members in the knowledge of the Word and in how to do the work of the ministry building up the Body of Christ.

4:13 When the gifts of the ministry are functioning correctly, the result will be the unity of faith, full understanding of the Word and an intimate relationship with Christ (Phil 3:8,10)

4:14 The ministry of the gifts within a church prevents instability in individuals and the deceivableness of error.

4:15 If we are following truth and communicating it with love, we are growing spiritually and numerically.

4:16 The force of a church is shown through the relationship among the members who are committed to mutually helping each other through their gifts.

B. The possible gifts mentioned in the passage

Gifts	Purpose	Genuine manifestation
Apostle	See 1 Corinthians 12	
Prophet	See Romans 12	
Evangelist	Enabled to teach and exhort the message of the gospel	Ability to clearly present the gospel in public or privately such that the message is understood and unbelievers are motivated to respond.
Pastor	Enabled to lead and care for the flock (believers) in Christ's church.	Ability to gain the "followship" of believers, leading them toward spiritual goals and protecting them from error
Teachers	See Romans 12	

IV. The principles of 1 Peter 4:7-11

*Technically speaking, there are no specific gifts mentioned in this passage, rather the context refers to basic categories of spiritual gifts: speaking and serving.

4:7 Since the end of time is near, we should invest our energies in eternal purposes that have high value for the kingdom.

4:8 The ministry among the believers should be motivated by love, which is evident by the mutually communicated protection and acceptance of one another. Faults and sins of each other are "overlooked" (1 Co 13:7), that is, not held up for criticism and rejection.

4:9 This characteristic is manifested by mutually meeting the needs of one another.

4:10 Each believer has received a special specific gift or ability and motivation to serve (*diakonia*) others, and they, in turn, are held accountable as stewards or administrators of fulfilling their particular ministry to others.

4:11 The spiritual gifts can be divided into two categories: gifts of speaking (i.e., evangelism, teaching, exhorting, wisdom) and gifts of serving (*diakonia*, i.e., helps, administration, mercy, giving, serving, leading, faith, discernment). The speaking gifts were always to be within the concepts and teachings of the Word already revealed ("the very words of God") and the service gifts were to be within the power given by God to give of oneself. The result would be that God is glorified, believers cannot live selfishly or egotistically for themselves, rather they are all motivated by the Spirit to sacrifice themselves as Christ in their service for others.

Four ways to analyze the gifts

I. In terms of how the gifts are exercised ("?" indicates possible temporary gifts)

The whole church	The church	dispursed	To both the church and unchurched	To the church at large
Prophecy	*To the unchurched*	*To believers*	Teaching	Apostle (?)
Knowledge	Mercy	Helps	Pastor	Evangelism
Wisdom	Evangelism	Faith	Wisdom	Teaching
Administration	Tongues (?)	Discernment	Knowledge	Exhorting
Giving	Interpretation (?)	Giving	Exhortation	Wisdom
Exhorting		Healing (?)	Apostle (?)	
Teaching			Evangelism	
Evangelism				

II. In terms of leadership and helping functions ("?" indicates possible temporary gifts)

Leadership		Auxilliary Functions	
Apostle	Helps, service	Giving	Tongues (?)
Teachers	Faith	Exhortation	Interpretation (?)
Pastor-teacher	Mercy	Administration	Healing (?)
Evangelist	Discernment	Knowledge (?)	Miracles (?)
Prophet (?)	Wisdom		
Leader			

III. In terms of what you can and cannot DEVELOP ("?" indicates possible temporary gifts)

Can be developed	Manifested already developed	Not clear
Teaching	Miracles (?)	Mercy
Pastor-teacher	Prophecy (?)	Administration
Wisdom, Knowledge	Tongues (?)	Leadership
Faith, Giving	Apostle (?)	
Evangelism	Tongues (?)	
Exhortation, Discernment	Interpretation (?)	

IV. In terms of focal emphasis

Speaking Gifts	Serving Gifts	Special Sign Gifts
Evangelism	Service, Helps	Miracles
Pastor-teacher	Giving	Healing
Teacher	Administration	Apostle
Exhortation	Leading	Tongues
Word of Knowledge	Showing Mercy	Interpretation
Word of Wisdom	Faith	Apostle
	Discernment	Prophecy

Description of the CARNAL and SATANIC false expression of the gifts

Carnal falsification	Satanic falsification
1. Apostle The determination to sacrifice your life by going into remote, dangerous places to become a "martyr" without sincerely seeking the will or wisdom of God. It is seeking fame.	Pious appearance, but brings false doctrine, ascetic self-denial and often powerful oratory (2 Cor 11:13; Rev 2:2).
2. Prophecy The preaching with seductive words of human wisdom depending on one's oratory, impression, emotionalism, sentimentalism and/or tactics of manipulation (1 Cor 2:1,4).	Preaching of false and deceiving doctrine without respect for the revealed Word of God, emphasizing new revelations and under the inspiration of evil spirits (1 Tim 1:6; 4:1).
3. Evangelism The use of human methods and psychology to produce "decisions" for God. It is noted for emotionalism and techniques to move the masses toward a decision whether they want to or not.	Directed by Satan to deceive people into believing they are saved through his false doctrine or no need to worry about it. Power to persuade with arguments not based on the Word, though it may be used.
4. Pastor A desire to lead for the glory of leadership fame or income. It is noted by human methods of improvement with an emphasis on social and material benefits, preoccupied with respect and acceptance from the world.	Motivated by Satan to deceive and to teach false and novel doctrine, denying the Scripture (as ancient), and exalting humanistic philosophies and personal views. They are totally closed to accepting biblical doctrines.
5. Teacher Emphasis on human wisdom, naturalistic philosophy and the success and well-being of man. It is dependent upon the personal capacity to persuade and for man to comprehend (Col 2:18; Rev 2:20)	Sensitive to seducing spirits, perhaps believing them to be of God, but resulting in false doctrine, usually attacking the Trinity, inspiration and biblical authority (1 Tim 4:1; 2 Cor 11:14, 15).
6. Wisdom The use of human wisdom and philosophy to adjust or explain the application of spiritual truth. Often relativistic and psychological (Acts 26:9; Rom 10:2).	The systems inspired by Satan to supposedly improve one's life or world, while following humanistic or satanic philosophies.
7. Knowledge The use of the Bible to promote secular ideas or secrets known only to the initiated, or humanistic philosophy clothed in biblical terminology.	The reception of supposed revelations, which add to the revealed Scripture, from the spirit world, while actually being seducing spirits (1 Tim 4:1).
8. Exhortation Efforts to help and counsel based on human wisdom, psychological theories and self-help themes, often to cover or ignore personal problems of guilt (Matt 16:22-23).	The satanically inspired counsel based on a seeking of spiritual powers, which result in immorality, rebellion and disobedience.

Carnal falsification	Satanic falsification
9. Faith A forced effort to believe in the supernatural, while depending on the human will and emotions or suggestions in order to accomplish some objective.	A confidence inspired by evil spirits, in occult powers from any source in order to accomplish an objective.
10. Discernment of spirits The effort of human wisdom to judge between what is of God or of Satan, based on human intuition and guessing.	The evil spirits discerning immediately what is of Christ and the ability to perceive what is a threat to Satan's objectives (Mr 3:11; 5:7; Acts 19:15; James 2:19).
11. Helps, service The material and humanitarian benefit of underprivileged for the motivation of feeling good about themselves or recognition of philanthropy.	Techniques of manipulation in order to attach followers to their false doctrines or movements that deny the Bible.
12. Giving The desire to be generous for selfish motivations (Acts 5).	Giving that is inspired by Satan to support works of deceiving and movements of error.
13. Leadership, administration Dependency on human capacity and techniques such as psychology of the masses, human manipulation and dominant personality.	The special capacity for dominance and power inspired by Satan in order to control others and accomplish his evil ends.
14. Mercy The acts of human kindness inspired by the noble philanthropy and caring, but limited by the strength of human love.	The supposed interest in human well-being but used as a means of deceiving and perverting (Gen 3:1, 4-5).
15. Miracles Natural phenomenon or coincidence attributed to divine intervention by religious enthusiasm, psychosomatic or suggestion	A special phenomenon produced by Satanic power to give credibility to false cults, spiritists or shamans.
16. Healing A physical change, real or imagined, resulting from psychosomatic suggestion attributed to divine intervention.	A physical transformation or appearance of change designed to exalt the power of Satan as used in certain false cults.
17. Tongues An ecstatic language produced by emotional powers accompanied by a forced excitation or faking of a supposed language, resulting in confusion, division and exalting of man	A language produced through a person under a spirit's control. Tend to fake spirituality, are erroneous and distracting from truth. Confirm error and division (1 Co 12:2-3).
18. Interpretation of tongues A faked or imagined interpretation of a supposed language from emotionalism and the motivation to prove a miracle occurred.	Evil spirits impress on a mind a supposed interpretation, faking the miraculous, and resulting in confirmation of false ideas.

A brief Historical Perspective of the Special Sign Gifts

The first two hundred years (100-300 AD)

A. The emphasis on the spiritual gifts was evident in the false movements of Gnosticism and in Montanism. The result of this false emphasis caused the Church to react critically against any who would seek to use the gifts. These groups emphasized the gift of prophecy, however, there is no documentation of any speaking in tongues. Montanus said that "after me there would be no more prophecy, but rather the end of the world" (Philip Schaff, *History of the Christian Church,* Vol II, p. 418). Since his prophecy was not fulfilled, it is obvious that he was a false prophet (Deut . 18:20-22). He said that he was the Comforter, the title of the Holy Spirit.

B. Hipolitus spoke a lot concerning the Holy Spirit and gifts. In his work called the *Apostolic Traditions* (215 AD) he made reference to a publication called "*Concerning the charismatic gifts*" that have been lost. The major problem of the Third century was the rise of a hierarchy between the clergy and a minimizing of the emphasis on the role of laity and their gifts. Hipolitus insisted on a major participation of laity and the use of their spiritual gifts.

C. Ireneus (died in 200 AD) and Origens (254 AD), both made references to spiritual gifts and especially to the problem of "tongues", but neither had seen the practice, but were writing what they had heard about it.

The next 1,200 years
(From the Council of Nicea to the Protestant Reformation 300-1500 AD)

A. The Bishop Ambrose of Milan (d. 397 AD) spoke briefly concerning "tongues" in his treatise "*Concerning the Spiritual Gifts*", in which he emphasized that every believer has a spiritual gift.

B. John Chrisostom (345-407 AD) of Constantinople referred to the theme of "*glossolalia*" as a scriptural event that had ceased. The occurrences of tongues was so distant from his experience that he describe it as "obscure" in the past.

C. San Augustine (354-430 AD), Bishop of Hipona in Africa, made reference to "tongues" and gifts. He said that tongues had disappeared very quickly in the Early Church.

D. The venerable Bede (d. 735 AD) made reference to the historical gift of tongues.

E. Thomas Aquinas (d. 1247 AD) wrote concerning the gift of tongues and believed that in his time it could be acquired through the study of linguistics.

F. The evidence of the Middle Ages show that there was very little emphasis in spiritual gifts. Some historians do make reference to the gift of "tongues." All of the people who supposedly spoke in tongues were saints of the Catholic Church. Such references were mentioned several hundred years after their deaths as proof of their sainthood, though there was never any actual contemporary evidence to confirm such reports. All the evidence of miracles during the Middle Ages is not trustworthy.

The next 400 years (from the Reformation to the 20th Century)
1500-1900 AD

A. Martin Luther (d. 1546 AD) said that the believers could receive one or various gifts of the Holy Spirit. He spoke of the fanaticism and the people that "wanted to be everything". He believed that "tongues" had been for a sign of the "testimony to the Jews."

B. John Calvin (d. 1564 AD) wrote extensively on the gift of tongues and believed that God had taken it from the church before it was adulterated with more abuses.

C. A renewal emphasis on the gifts began with the appearance of the dualists Camisares or the Prophets of the Mountains and the Cevenoles of France (1702-1705 AD). They were sure that the prophecy of Joel was being fulfilled in their age. They said that voices from heaven spoke to them, that stars guided them and that wounds would not do them harm. They cried tears of blood. They practiced speaking ecstatically giving prophecies, at times in convulsions and foaming at the mouth. Prophets supposedly spoke in Latin, Hebrew, French and other dialects. They said that Christ was to return soon.

D. The Jansenites left the Roman Catholic Church in a time of persecution. They rejected the doctrine of the justification by faith, insisting on a personal experience of their soul with their Creator, with such a relationship only possible in and by the Roman Catholic Church. Their movement was characterized by prophets even from childhood, convulsions, people given to ecstasies beyond control of themselves and unintelligible expressions while being unconscious (not pretending that this was speaking in tongues). They remained loyal to the Roman Church.

E. The Anabaptist Radicals (one of four grups of Anabaptists) in Germany were a faction of the larger Anabaptist movement (a rebaptism movement), that followed the practices of the Jansenites. They declared Strasburg to be the New Jerusalem and their leader as the king of the Kingdom. They practiced polygamy. They proclaimed many false prophecies, but there was no evidence of speaking in tongues or miracles.

F. Edward Irving (d. 1834 AD), a Scotch Presbyterian, began preaching a movement of restoration of the spiritual gifts for the Church. The Irvingites of England sought the gift of tongues. Their church had apostles, prophets and those that spoke in tongues. The prophets said that their declarations were "inspired." The movement formed the Apostolic Catholic Church with altars, robes for their ministers, extreme unction, transubstantiation, incense, blessed water and other practices of the Catholic Church.

G. The Shakers, begun by Ann Lee Stanley (d. 1784 AD), practiced the gifts of the Spirit and seemed to have roots in the Camisares. They were extremely fanatical and demonstrative in the use of the gifts. They rejected the Trinity, the bodily resurrection and the expiation or payment for sins. They did not adore Jesus. They believed that it was possible to communicate with the spiritual world, that all the world has a second opportunity to accept salvation in the next life and that to live without sin was an obligation. At times they danced nude. The goal of the cult was to experience ecstasy loosing control of themselves, dancing, jumping and expressing unintelligible things. The exalted their own "inner light" more than the Bible.

H. John Wesley (d. 1791 AD) did not claim to have any special gift, but is seen as the "Father" of the Pentecostal movement because he preached the second work of grace. In some of his meetings, people fell as dead, mumbling things without sense. Such experiences were not limited to believers, rather, were common among unbelievers who attended. Thus, these were not spiritual gifts. There is not evidence of speaking in tongues in his campaigns.

I. The Mormons (Joseph Smith, d. 1844 AD) believed and practiced the gifts of the Spirit, especially that of tongues.

The 20th Century (since 1900 AD to present)

A. Modern Pentecostalism was initiated by Charles F. Parham in Topeka, Kansas, New Years, 1901 AD

B. In 1905, Parham moved to Houston, Texas, where he met an African-American, William Seymour. Seymour moved to Los Angeles in 1906 and began the famous Revival of Azusa Street.

C. In 1910 the denomination of the Pentecostals of the Apostolic Faith was founded and in 1914 the Assemblies of God.

D. Pentecostalism grew rapidly in all the world through the Holiness Movement, already a worldwide influence. The similarity of doctrine made it a natural union, that is, the doctrines of the second work of grace and the baptism of the Spirit for the power to grow in sanctification. Finney, Moody, Simpson, Keswick and Chapman all contributed to the development of Pentecostalism through their emphasis on the Baptism of the Spirit for power to be sanctified without a focus on tongues.

E   On April 3, 1960, Father Dennis Bennett, Rector of the Episcopal Church of Van Nuys, Calif., announced that he had spoken in tongues. This marked the beginning of the Neo-Pentecostal Movement or the Charismatic Movement, in which all denominations have participated or have been affected. The current interest in the Roman Catholic Church is the continuing importance of the Charismatic Movement.

F. The Pentecostal Movement is basically responsible for special emphasis in the 20th Century on "spiritual gifts," especially the gifts of tongues and healing over the lesser emphasis given to the other gifts.

G. The general theme of the Gifts of the Spirit is capturing the interest of many churches and leaders. Many books and articles have appeared on this these and have had influence in the presentation of this present study.

H. The fundamental act that has affected interest in Spiritual Gifts is the depersonalization of the secular society and the desire of people to know their dignity and value. In the local church, the questions are often: Are we interested in people? Are lay people necessary in the growth and ministry of the church? The answer is a resounding, "Yes!"

A historical perspective

A   The use of spiritual gifts is reduced to insignificance when the role of lay people is minimized.

B. The lack of biblical teaching in the Middle Ages is the reason for our failure to comprehend and know how to utilize the spiritual gifts.

C. Fanaticism and emotional exibitionalism in the use of the spiritual gifts have been associated often with false doctrine and sects. They have discouraged the churches from identifying the need and benefit of the spiritual gifts.

D. When the role of the clergy advanced towards assuming the ministries described by the spiritual gifts, the use of these gifts on the part of the laity, as also the desire to use them, diminishes.

E. The understanding and use of the spiritual gifts prospers under the encouragement and teaching of the leaders of the church. The responsibility rests on their shoulders!

F. The exalting of certain gifts over others tends to diminish the importance of the lesser gifts, and produces extremism and lack of balance in the ministry of the local church.

Section II:

A Definition of the Gifts of the Spirit

A Study of the Definitions and Symptoms of the Gifts

Introduction

The Bible does not define the different gifts. It uses various phrases to convey their meanings, in different contexts it shows how they are to be used and finally, it illustrates them in the lives of gifted people. In most cases all believers are expected to perform the activities (or working out) of all of the gifts as they learn how to serve others by observing those people specifically gifted in each area. Some of the gifts are not even mentioned outside the lists given in the Scriptures. Obviously then, a definition of the gifts will require considerable interpretation and certain amplitude allowing for a variety of opinions.

Some of the gifts are declared by Paul to be of a temporary nature (prophecy, knowledge, and tongues, 1 Cor 13:8), so the natural question is, when? If we can establish that those gifts had a temporary purpose in the foundation period of the Church, it is possible that there were other gifts that were not going to be permanent for the whole Church Age: apostleship, healing, interpretation of tongues and miracles. Some include in this list of temporary gifts the Word of Wisdom, Discernment of Spirits and the gift of Faith (if it is to do miracles).

On the other hand, some want all of the gifts to be operative today just as they were in the NT era. This view sees all the gifts functioning in the apostolic form until the Second Coming of Christ, then they will cease. A clear interpretation of 1 Cor 13:8 will determine which of these views is most biblica.

The reality is in the strictest sense, Apostles such as Paul and Peter do not exist in the contemporary Church. Their authority, privileges of special, infallible revelation and powers to confirm the validity of their message of salvation (Heb 2:3-4) made them a very unique group with a defined and limited duration and purpose.

Those who insist in the continued existence of the gift of apostle are divided into two camps: (1) those who believe that there are no differences between those who claim to be "apostles" of today and those of the Early Church. They insist that the contemporary "missionaries" must manifest the "signs of an apostle" (2 Cor 12:12) and thus, have the same authority. (2) Others distinguish between the office and the gift of apostle. They believe that the office belonged exclusively to the thirteen apostles in the NT, but contend that today the gift of apostle is manifested in the capacity to be effective as a missionary in another culture extending the Church to new people groups.

There are two gifts that tend to be interpreted in this contemporary fashion: apostleship and prophecy. The problem with this interpretation is that the Bible nowhere indicates a distinction between the gift and the office. Apostolically gifted men (1 Cor 12:29) were given to the church as apostles (Eph 4:11) and prophetically gifted persons (1 Cor 12:10) were given to the church as prophets (Eph 4:11), but there is no distinction between the original gift and the original function in the Early Church. Every apostle and every prophet in the NT acts consistently with the original sense of the meaning of their gifts.

The word *apostoloi* included more than the original 13 in four or five contexts. However, no one suggests that the other companions of the Apostles had authority equal to the original 13. A careful examination of these texts will show a variety of possible interpretations, which must result in harmony with all the other Scriptural and historical evidence.

There were others who claimed the apostolic gift as well as the same authority as the apostle Paul, if not more so. However, they were the cause of division and conflicts in the Early Church (2 Co 11:13; Rev 2:2) and they were all rejected. If they had not been personally elected by Jesus to be an apostle they were rejected in the Early Church.

If there still existed in the Church some form of the gifts of apostle and of prophet, they would be as "missionary" and "preacher", but these two manifestations can be explained more practically by the gift-clusters of evangelist, exhorter, teacher or pastor-teacher.

Definitions of the Gifts

The approach that will be followed in the analysis of the gifts will be the following:

1. A linguistic definition for the use of the gift's title in different ages:
   a. The definitions will include the uses of the word in the period of Classical Greek (Homer, Socrates, Demosthenes, etc.) or approximately 800-400 BC when pertenent.
   b. Definitions will be given from the age of the Old Testament as seen in the Septuagint (LXX or the Greek translation of the Hebrew OT) around 250 BC
   c. Definitions from the age of the New Testament (50-100 AD) will be given.
   d. Additional uses of the word in the NT text and the Early Church Age literature when helpful.
2. There will be an explanation of the use of the word in different contexts as it is used today.
3. Included will be a list of possible symptoms deduced from the meaning of the words and practical observations of the gifts that are common in the ministry today. This phase of the definition is obviously very subjective, not universal and is included only to help to discern what God perhaps is writing on the pages of our hearts and minds to help us desire to do His will (Phil 2:13).

As you study each gift there should be an affinity or attraction to certain gifts. You will think, "This is what I really want to do" or "This is describing my feelings." You should take note of those gifts for further focus and practice in different ministries.

1. Apostle

A. Definition:

1. The study of the word meaning (81 times in the NT. Only 3 times does not refer to the 12)

Greek	Etymology	Translation	Basic Idea	Passages
apostolos	apo- "outside -stello "put in order"	apostle (131 times)	Someone sent to act on behalf of another with his full authority. It is someone commissioned.	Heb. 3:1 Luke 6:13
		messenger (could be an angel) or a "sent one"	Emissary, agent to fulfill a specific task.	Acts 14:4, 14 Rom 16:7; 2 Cor 8:23 John 13:16; Phil 2:25

2. In the Classics the word signified someone sent with all the power and authority of the one who sent him. That person was a representative with an intimate connection, which was enviable. It is used in the context of mariners with cargo ships. It is used of a command of sailors sent to other countries. Thus the term has two concepts: (1) a special commission, (2) a sending overseas.

3. It is used 700 times as a verb in the LXX, to translate the Hebrew *salah*, "send with a purpose, with authority." Another Greek verb for "send" is *pempo* (5 times in the LXX) is used to indicate only "being sent." However, the Hebrew word *saliah* could indicate someone who took the place of a bridegroom in a wedding. The term is limited normally to being sent for one purpose (i.e. to bring the offering of the synagogue to Jerusalem), not to a permanent office.

4. In the NT it is used as a verb 131 times (119 in the gospels and Acts). As a noun it appears 76 times, principally in the writings of Luke (62 times). With two exceptions it is used by Luke to refer to the twelve.

B. Explanation

1. What we learn from the writings of Paul can be summarized as following: (1) It is a life-long commission received directly from the Lord Jesus in person (1 Cor 15:7, 8; Gal 1:16-17); (2) It is the responsibility to go to the Gentiles (Rom 11:13; Gal 2:8), originally in twos (Gal 2:1, 9; Mark 6:7; Acts 15:36-40; 2 Cor 4:7-12), to preach, but not to baptize (1 Cor 1:17); (3) It was inevitable that they were going to suffer severely (1 Cor 4:9-13; 15:30; 2 Cor 4:7-12); (4) It was not to be considered a specially elevated position (1 Cor 4:16; Phil 3:17), any more so than other members of the church (1 Cor 12:25-28; Eph 4:11), rather it was to complete a special function in the foundation of the Early Church (Eph 2:20); (5) Paul made it clear that he was the last of the apostles that saw the Lord (1 Cor 15:8), thus it would be impossible that there would be more apostles called by the Lord as the twelve and Paul.

2. The Latin word for *apostolos* is "*misio*", from which is transliterated the English word "mission-ary." Some have wanted to insist in the difference between the GIFT and the OFFICE. The office of apostle terminated with the Twelve and Paul. They had the responsibility and min-istry of testifying about the resurrection, establishing the correct foundational doctrine of the Church (Eph 2:20; Acts 2:42) and were confirmed in that unique authority through miracles and signs (Mark 16:9-20; Heb 2:3-4). Today we take their confirmed evidence as sufficient to base our faith upon their words.

3. The question remains, is the apostolic gift continuing in the church as the "gift of missionary," or is there a renewal of the apostolic gift? The argument for this interpretation is based on the number of persons included below the title "apostle" that appears to extend beyond the Twelve plus Paul.

   a. When someone accompanied an apostle, the group customarily was called collectively the "apostles", such as "Paul and Barnabas" (Acts 14:4, 14). However, nowhere is Barnabas ever considered an apostle independently of Paul.
   b. Silas and Timothy are grouped together with Paul (1 Thess 1:1) and considered "apostles" (2:6), but only in association with Paul. He had called both of them to join his "apostolic group" and had delegated to them his apostolic authority for special commissions, but nowhere are they considered authoritarian apart from Paul, nor permanently given that position in the Church. Apostles apparently could not delegate their ultimate authority to another.
   c. The expression in Gal 1:19 would appear to include James in the apostolic grouping, but the verse can be taken both ways. It is not a clear expression. Nowhere else is James con-sidered an apostle.
   d. The statement of Paul referring to two men who were famous "among the apostles," in Rom 16:7, "Andronicus and Junia, my kinsmen, and my fellow prisoners, who are *of note among* the apostles, who also were in Christ before me." The phrase "of note among" translates, *episemos*, "well known, marked in a good sense" by the apostles. The expression again is relatively ambiguous; it can be taken several ways. It could mean that they were included among the twelve apostles (doubtful) or that they were highly respected by all the Twelve (more likely).
   e. The term "apostles of the churches" as distinct from the phrase "apostles of Jesus" is a term, which referred to Titus (2 Cor 8:23) and to Epaphroditus (Phil 2:25). It is possible

that the term referred to a person sent by a church with a specific purpose (to take an offering to the Jerusalem church) or to a ministry that the church wanted to fulfill (to serve Paul). In the case of Titus and others, they were already sent by Paul with apostolic authority, but this did not indicate that they were independently considered apostles, rather that they were acting with the authority of an apostle. In both cases, the term referred to a temporary and specific mission.

4. Someone with the gift of apostle possessed many, if not the majority of the spiritual gifts: sign gifts (Acts 5:12-16), miracles (Acts 13:8-11), prophecy (Acts 27:25) and tongues (Acts 2:4; 1 Cor 14:18). All were given to prove their apostleship (2 Cor 12:12) and to validate the message of salvation Jesus came to offer. This would make no sense if everyone or many were to have the sign gifts. Since they were to be the instruments that God would utilize for the revelation of the New Testament, probably as well had the gifts of the word of wisdom and word of knowledge (1 Cor 2:7, 10, 13; 2 Pet 3:15-16) and as orators of the new revelation given them, they manifested the gift of prophecy (Rev 1:1-3).

With all this, even the apostles were never considered infallible in their oratory or actions. Only when they would write the revelation of God under the inspiration of God could they produce something infallible and without error: the inspired Word of God. It should be noted, that the apostolic and prophetic authors were not inspired, only their writings were inspired.

5. How should the work of "missionary" be fulfilled today? The gifts of evangelism, exhortation, pastor and teacher are more than adequate to realize the work of the expansion of the church throughout the world. The expansion of the church works, not under modern apostolic authority, but rather under the authority of the apostolic Word of God delivered to the church in the first century that is now proclaimed in the power of the gospel (Rom 1:16) and willing witness, disciple-makers and teachers who follow the apostolic example planting churches in every corner of the world.

2. Prophet

A. Definition

1. A study of the word (148 times in the NT)

Greek	Etymology	Translation	Basic Ideas	Passages
propheteuo	*pro-* "before" *-phemi* "to say or declare;"	prophet	Predict the future openly and publicly, pronounce the Word of God given by the Spirit for the church. Always results in exhortation, edification and comfort to the believers.	Acts 21:9-11; 11:27-30; Titus 1:12; 1 Cor 14:3-4; Acts 15:32

2. In the Classics it did not have the sense of foreknowledge until later. The use of the word does not express the basic idea of the etymology of the word. The idea was one who proclaimed publicly the will or words of another.

3. In the OT, the prophet, *nabi*, (meaning "to proclaim or call; or divulge, make known") was a preacher or announcer of God's revelation. The noun appears 309 times (92 times in Jeremiah). Various persons were called prophets (Abraham: Gen 20:7; Moses: Dt 34:10; Aaron: Ex 7:1; David: Neh 12;24, 36). The use suggests an intimate relationship with God such that God could speak directly to him or through him. The sense is an "interpreter" or "one through whom God speaks." Thus the prophet proclaimed the Word of God received by revelation for the purposes of warning, exhorting, consoling, teaching and counseling. The "false prophet" was evident when he "prophesied" an event that did not occur (Dt. 18:18). When God spoke through a prophet He never made a mistake.

4. In the NT the word appears 148 times; it is used as a verb 28 times. The basic sense is the proclamation of divine revelation (Mat 7:22) bringing comfort or providing exhortation and teaching (1 Cor 14:3, 31). The term "false prophet" in the NT does not indicate that their predictions did not come to pass, but rather that their teachings were not in agreement with those of the apostles (1 Cor 14:29; Acts 2:42). They pretended to speak for God, but He had not told them what they were saying (Jer14:14).

The believers that were prophets in the Early Church participated in the meetings (1 Cor 14:24), were obligated to make their proclamations in understandable words (1 Cor 12:1; 14:15, 23) and had to speak by turns (1 Cor 14:30-31). A genuine prophet never lost control of himself (1 Cor 14:32), rather was submissive to order and peace in the congregation (14:33).

The prophet contributed an integral part in the "foundation" of the Church (Eph 2:20), which would suggest a temporary nature to the gift, fulfilling its purpose when all the foundational revelation necessary for confirming and establishing the Church had been revealed through its unique function.

The gift of prophecy in the NT has less emphasis on the predictive element as compared to the use of prophecy in the OT, but it was still evident (Acts 11:27-28; 21:10-11; Rev 1:3). The culmination of the final prophetic utterance in the Book of Revelation strongly suggests that prophecy was terminating with the conclusion of the Revelation (22:18).

5. After the first century, the emphasis on the continuance of the gift of prophecy led to the sect called Montanism. Montanus said that he was the prophet of God and his followers were called "spiritual." In spite of some good ideas they were excommunicated from the church for their excesses.

B. Explanation

1. Once again some want to make a distinction between the gift and the office of prophecy. It is an appealing concept, but nowhere is it suggested in Scripture. The idea that the office was realized in the NT and ended, but the proclamation aspect of the gift continues in the Church as preachers sounds interesting.   Paul, however, declared that the prophecy in the Early Church was piecemeal, that is, it could only declare "in part" or a portion of the whole revelation, which God would eventually complete (1 Cor 13:9-10). The prophet did not determine what he wanted to say, but rather was dependent upon revelation from God. There was no study, no preparation or planning involved because the message was revealed supernaturally (1 Cor 14:30). Though some would claim that their spontaneous preaching is the same thing, interpreting Spirit-given impressions to be revelations from God's Word can be deceiving.

2. The function of prophecy in the Early Church was reemphasized through the gift of evangelism, teaching and exhorting in the congregations. These functions all utilize the product of the gift of prophecy, as the Early Church "persevered in the doctrine of the apostles" (Acts 2:42). The priority of the gift of prophecy in 1 Cor 14 was not that of the gift itself, but the ministry was fulfilled by the use of the message of prophecy in the church for "edification, exhortation and comfort" (1 Cor 14:3) and evangelism (14:24-25). Now these very functions are continued in the church by continual use of previously revealed divine messages from God, through the exercise of other gifts (teaching, exhorting, comforting, etc.) that are to be given priority in the church.

3. Evangelism

A. Definition:

1. Study of the word (3 times as a noun - evangelist)

Greek	Etymology	Translation	Basic Idea	Passages
euangelististes	eu- "good" -angello "announcement"	evangelize proclaim preach	Announce "good new;" bring news that causes rejoicing	Acts 21:8; Eph 4:11 Heb 5:42; 8:4, 12, 25; 8:35, 40
euangelion	eu- "good" -angelos "messenger"	evangelist	A proclaimer of good news	Acts 15:7; Gal 3:8

2. In the Classics, the term was used for a messenger who carried the report of a victory or other political or personal news that would cause rejoicing. The person that received the report would go out immediately and offer sacrifices of gratitude to the gods as a result of his joy.

3. In the OT (LXX), it translated bissar, "announce, publicize" the fulfillment of the prophecy of the universal victory of the kingdom of God (Isa 52:7). The proclamation of the kingdom was announced with great joy (Isa 40:9; Psalms 96:2).

4. In the NT, as a noun, the word appears 60 times in the writing of Paul. As a verb it signified the proclamation of salvation by grace for persons who could never merit such an acceptance by God, with the end result being that many would accept the message. The term "evangelist" is very rare in non-Christian literature, but is common in early Christian literature. The NT refers to Philip (Acts 21:8) as an "evangelist" and to the "evangelists" that God gives to the local churches (Eph 4:11). In 2 Tim 4:5 Timothy and we are all exhorted to do the work of an evangelist.

B. Explanation

1. The content of the message of an evangelist, the "gospel," has power in itself to bring conviction of sin and salvation (Rom 1:16; 1 Cor 15:2), but also judgment (Rom 2:16). It is to reveal God in His righteousness (Rom 1:17) and produce hope (Col 1:5, 23) and peace (Eph 2:17; 6:15) in the believer. The message should produce new life (1 Pet 1:23-25) with the result that the power of His life resides in the spirit of man through the Word of God (1 Pet 1:12). It is deposited in the life of the believer with great confidence (2 Ti 1:10-11). The model of proclaiming the message is given (Rom 10:15) in order to be directed to every social class, culture, race or nation (Eph 3:1-9) with the end result being their salvation (Eph 1:13). Who would not want to share a message that produces such results?

2. If the belief is correct that the position of apostle was fulfilled in the first century, then the continuance of the expansion of the church is to be carried out by evangelists throughout the Church Age (2 Tim 4:5), following the ministry model of the apostles.

3. It is the capacity and passion to present the gospel with such clarity and conviction that the unconverted tend to respond by opening their hearts to the Lord. The effectiveness of the gift is seen in the Parable of the Sower, showing the unbeliever "understanding" the message (Mt

13:19, 23) in which he is asked to trust with all his heart. An example is seen in Acts 8:26-39.

4. It is the capacity to motivate by personal example and exhortation, and to train others in evangelism in the local church (Eph 4:11-12).

5. Some church analysts have estimated that statistically an average of approximately 10% of a congregation should have the gift of evangelist, in order to motivate the continual emphasis in the activities of the church.

C. Symptoms

1. The first symptom of the gift is the passion or burden to see others coming to know Christ as their personal Savior. It is a recurring thought that does not go away. The evangelist sees everyone in the light of whether they are saved or lost.

2. The liberty and boldness to speak with ease before either groups or individuals concerning the message of salvation. It seems natural to turn the conversation to spiritual themes that end up being a presentation of the gospel.

3. The result is the capacity to persuade or influence others for Christ. It is not forced, rather is easy and natural to persuade others to accept Christ.

4. It is a capacity to meet new people, form new friendships with unbelievers, gain their confidence and provoke their interest in the things of God.

5. It is natural to pray for unbelievers by name, or lift up specific groups of people or nations to the Lord in prayer, asking for the open door for someone to preach the gospel with power to everyone.

4. Pastor

A. Definition

1. Study of the words related to the subject

Greek	Etymology	Translation	Basic Idea	Passage
presputero	*presb-* "old"	"elder"	Mature, respectable, wise	Acts 20:17-28
episkopo	*epi-* "over" *-skopos* "look with great care"	"bishop, watcher, overseer" -- someone responsible for others	Responsibility for the care of the flock	1 Tim 3:1-8
poimaino	*pimne-* "flock"	"pastor"	Care for, protect, govern, lead, nurture, feed, mature	1 Pet 5:1-11
prosistemi	*pro-* "before" *-istemi* "stand"	"to go before, to preside, lead, direct"	To be in front, direct, preside, manage, conduct, lead, initiative taker.	Rom 12:8; 1 Tim 3:4, 5, 12; 5:17
hegemon	"leader"	"ruler, governor, leader"	The one that provides, thinks, orders, plans, maintains, disciplines	Heb 13:7, 17, 24; Acts 23:24; 26:30
didaskalos	See next gift discription			

2. The word for pastor, *poimne*, is used metaphorically in the Classics in reference to a leader, a governor or commander. It carries the idea of someone who takes care a flock under his protection. His devotion to meet the needs and protect his followers at all costs is the heart of his leadership.

3. God is called the Shepherd of Israel who goes before the flock (Ps. 68:7), guides it (Ps. 23:3), leads it to food and water (Ps. 23:2), protects it (Ps. 23:4), and carries its young (Is. 40:11). Embedded in the living piety of believers, the metaphor brings out the fact that people are sheltered in God. In the LXX, Jehovah is the only pastor of the flock of Israel (Psalms 23; 28:9; 68:8; 74:1; 77:20; 78:52; Jer 23:2; 31:10), but later became the official title that was given to the king, as an expression of honor (2 Sam 5:2; 1 Chron 11:2; 2 Sam 24:17).

4. The prophets denounced the "pastors" (leaders) of the nation (Jer 2:8; 3:15; Isa 56:11). When Cirus, King of Persia, authorized the restoration of Jerusalem from captivity, God gave him the title "My pastor" (Isa 44:28). In Jeremiah the term is applied to political and military rulers, but not as a title. The shepherds have proved unfaithful; hence God himself will take up the office and appoint better shepherds (Jer. 3:15; 23:4). He will set up one shepherd who will reunite the people, the Messiah (Ezek. 34:23-24; 37:22, 24).

5. In the NT the devotion of a pastor is praised (Jn 10:3; Lk 15:4). Pastors are exhorted not to be

selfish, but to be servants of the flock meeting their needs (1 Pet 5:2-4; Acts 20:28). The example to follow is that of the Pastor of pastors, the Lord Jesus (1 Pet 5:4). "As a pastor, he cares for the flock. He guides, guards, protects, and provides for those under his oversight." An example is found in Acts 20:28 where Paul exhorts the elders from Ephesus "to shepherd the church of God." The key to the value of the church is the following phrase, "which He bought with His own blood." It is to be done voluntarily, not for material gain or by lording it over believers but rather by being examples of humility (1 Pet. 5:2–5).

B. Explanation

1. The gifted pastor in the context of Ephesians 4:11 speaks of one of four or five classes of men who have been uniquely gifted by the Spirit to fulfill special functions of leadership in the Body of Christ and specifically in the local church. It is the only "gift" that is described in details including requirements, attitudes and desires of the recipient. It is possible to have the desire to be a pastor, but not have matured sufficiently to fulfill the ministry of a pastor.

2. The term "pastor" is a synonym of two other terms for describing the church leadership: bishop (*episkopo*) and elder (*presbutero*). In Acts 20:17, 28, the "elders" (*presbuteros*) should take great care of themselves and the flock which "the Holy Spirit has made you overseers (*episkopos*). To be shepherds (*poimaino*) of the church of God." Each term is a description of different aspects of the function of a gifted pastor in a local church. In Titus 1:5, 7 the "elders" and "bishops" are likewise interchanged.

C. Symptoms

1. It is the capacity to exercise influence over a group leading them to a specific goal or purpose, or to make decisions. People tend to look to a pastor for leadership (He has a track record of being the president of organizations, clubs, etc)

2. The gift produces the capacity to provoke a "follow-ship"; others want to follow his leadership because of the confidence that his relationship with them has generated. They are convinced that he will not use or abuse them, but rather, their spiritual and emotional needs will be met as they follow his leadership.

3. He has the capacity to maintain order and discipline in whatever group he may belong to.

4. He tends to see the problems in a group as a realist and yet is willing to take responsibility for helping them through their problems even at personal risk.

5. His passion that Christians grow in their knowledge of Christ and His word, in unity and in their obedience to what they know of the Word is evident. He is genuinely concerned for the well being of his followers.

6. His influence and example tends to produce a loyalty toward his person, his manner of thinking and his values in life.

7. From deep within, this person longs to take responsibility for the church people that Christ paid for with His own blood. There is nothing more precious to the Savior.

5. Teacher

A. Definition:

1. Study of the word and associated words

Greek	Etymology	Translation	Basic Idea	Passages
didaskalos	*dek-* "accept, extend a helping hand"	"teacher"	Someone who leads another to accept new concepts: INSTRUCTION	Matt 5-7; Jn 6:59; Acts 18:11; 1 Tim 2:2
manthano	*math-* "adapt"	"learner, disciple;" learn from instruction	Adapt the thinking to the will of another: ACQUIRER	Mtt 11:29; 28:19; Acts 14:21
diermeneuo	*dia-* emphasis *-hermeneuo*, "interpret"	"interpreter, translator; explain"	Make clear or explain the truth: EXPLANATION	Matt 24:27; 1 Cor 12:3; 30
eksegeomai	*ek-* "out" *segeomai*, "lead" thus "draw out; unfold"	"explain, expose; make fully known"	Clarify difficulties; interpret the will of God: EXPOSITION	John 1:18; Acts 10:8; Luke 24:35
dialogizomai	*dia-* "through" *-logizomai*, "converse" thus "think thru, discuss"	"Think, reason, give an opinion, discuss, consider, teacher"	Something discovered through logical reasoning: PERSUASION	Acts 19:9, 10; Heb 12:5

2. The gift of teaching is the ability to instruct, explain and present Biblical truths in such a manner that believers understand the Scriptures and incorporate the truth into their personal lives. Instruction in the truths of the faith is a priority for the church (1 Cor 14:19). All the apostles and prophets were continually involved in teaching (Ac 18:11; 19:9-10; Col 1:28; 1 Ti 1:11; 2:2 7). In the categories of the gifts (1 Cor 12:28), teaching is third in the list behind apostle and prophet.

3. In Classical Greek the word is common from Homer, denoting the act of teaching and learning in the wide sense of imparting theoretical and practical knowledge with the highest development of the pupil being the goal. There is little religious use and the term has a strong intellectual and authoritative bearing. Thus it can also mean, "to demonstrate." When used in connection with choral training, it comes almost to have the sense, "to perform."

4. The term occurs some 100 times in the LXX (mostly for the root). While various kinds of instruction can be meant (cf. 2 Sam. 22:35; Dt. 31:19), understanding God's will is the special object, with a volitional as well as an intellectual reference. This is distinct from secular usage, where the aim is to develop talents; the OT relates teaching to the totality of the person.

5. In the NT the word *didasko* appears 95 times and signifies a communication skill of imparting knowledge to another. Jesus "taught" the Pharisees (Mr 10:1; 12:14). He had a balance between the interpretation of the truth and the application in lives (Mr 6:2, 34). In addition He practiced the concept of teaching evangelism (Mr 1:15; Ac 4:2, 18; 5:28, 42). Practically there was little difference between preaching and teaching the gospel (Ac 18:11, 25, 28; 28:31). The message of the gospel was proved trustworthy through teaching the OT (Ac 1:1; 4:18; 5:12, 25, 28, 42; 11:26; 15:1, 35; 20:20).

6. Timothy was commanded to teach (1 Ti 4:11; 6:2) and transmit the apostolic teaching to other "faithful men" (2 Tim 2:2), a special group of restricted men. This was probably part of the process in developing elders or pastors, who had to be *didaktikos*, "capable of teaching" (1 Ti 3:2, 2 Tim 2:24). This would imply a preparation to be able to teach and defend the faith.

7. It should be noted that the only restriction from teaching is that women are prohibited from teaching men or assuming authority (through teaching) over men (1 Tim 2:12) in the congregation. There is no restriction for women teaching other women and children, in fact they are commanded to do so in Titus 2:3-5.

8. It appears that there were various levels of leadership in the Early Church: apostles and prophets, when they existed, had priority. Later came the Teacher (1 Cor 12:28) and forth, the Evangelist. In the *Didache* (13:2), the leaders of the churches were prophets and teachers.

9. Teaching did not involve any special revelation, oral or written, rather the ability deals with communication skills and motivation to make self-evident or understandable the truth already revealed. Prophecy is a priority because of the authoritarian revelation from God, though all prophets must be compared to and subject to the apostles. Once revealed the teacher is to continually clarify every revelation.

B. Explanation

1. There are four concepts in the definition of the gift of teaching:
   a. Supernatural ability
   b. Clear communication
   c. Effective application
   d. Understanding of the truth of the Word already revealed

2. It is one of the most important gifts since it appears in 3 of the 4 lists of the gifts (as also prophecy). Exhortations and preaching are based on the teachings.

3. The spiritual results are the spreading of the Word in the world (Ac 19:9, 10) and also evangelism (20:20; 21:28).

4. Teaching appears to be a general goal for everyone as a part of the expected maturity (Heb 5:12). Every believer should prepare himself to be a teacher.

5. The responsibility of being a teacher has its own risk (James 3:1) because of the constant speaking, it becomes easy to exaggerate, communicate mistruths and make errors in the use of the Scriptures.

6. The purpose of teaching is the maturity of others (Col 1:28).

7. The principle danger for teachers is PRIDE of their knowledge or exaggerated desire to be respected by their students and the tendency to DISCREDIT or CRITIZE others of lesser ability.

8. The ministry of teaching is normally oriented toward the congregation, though small groups are insinuated in 2 Tim 2:2. In the leadership roles the capability to teach is required, though some probably will not have the motivation (gift) to excel in the ministry of preparing and teaching (1 Ti 5:17). A major part of the responsibility of Timothy was teaching (1 Tim 4:11; 6:2).

C. Symptoms

1. The true teacher is blessed with an ease of understanding the Bible and great motivation to study. Personal satisfaction from having applied the principles of the Bible to his personal life generates a desire to impart the benefits and blessings to other lives.

2. The teacher constantly accumulates knowledge and has special discipline for studying the Word in depth. He is not satisfied with uncertain explanations, rather wants to confirm the veracity of ideas and concepts. Normally he is suspicious of new ideas and concepts until they are proven from Scriptures.

3. A teacher loves to systematically organize details and illustrate them graphically.

4. He believes that individuals will become more like Christ in character and maturity as they understand more about the character and will of God, Christ and the Spirit, committing themselves to obey and imitate His qualities. Teaching is the link in the process giving believers the understanding necessary and orientation towards how to apply the understanding gained for their personal lives.

6. Exhortation

A. Definition

1. A study of the word and associated words

Greek	Etymology	Translation	Basic Ideas	Passages
parakaleo	para- "alongside" kaleo, "call"	"exhort, admonish, console encourage"	To speak directly to someone, to urge, beg, encourage, or strengthen.	1 Thes 4:1; 5:14; 2 Thes 3:12; 1 Tim 2:1; 6:2; Heb 3:13
noutheto	nous- "mind" -tithemi, "to put"	"to impart understanding, to lay on the heart."	To warn, instruct, remind, correct	Rom 15:14; 1 Thes 5:12; 2 Thes 3:15; Col 3:16; Acts 20:31
paideuo	pais- "child"	"instruct, train, chasten, correct, whip, scourge"	Training of children, who need direction, teaching and discipline	Acts 7:22; 22:3; 1 Cor 11:32; 1 Tim 1:20; 2 Tim 2:25; Heb 12:6-10
elegcho	"expose"	"convict, refute, reprove, rebuke, find fault with"	Prove or test a thing, bring to contempt or shame, expose guilt to motivate repentance	Eph 5:11, 13; 2 Tim 4:2; Titus 1:9

Greek	Etymology	Translation	Basic Ideas	Passages
dialegomai	*dia-* "through" *lego-* "talk"	"think, reason, give an opinion, discuss, consider"	Direction of one's thinking, discuss, ponder, resolve in mind, discourse, dispute with questions	Acts 17:2, 17; 18:4, 19 19:8-9; 10; 20:7,9; 24:12; Heb 12:5

2. Exhortation is the capacity to encourage others to act according to the correct application of the Biblical truths, or to console others from the promises of Scripture.

3. In the OT (LXX), the word *parakaleo*, was used to translate the Hebrew *naham*, "be moved to pity, to comfort or console" (Psa 119:50; Gen 37:35). Part of the responsibility of the prophet was to produce comfort (Isa 40:1). It also has the sense of encouragement and strengthening (Dt 3:28:Job 4:3) or to guide in the way (Ex 15:13). It is a very positive term as in the phrase "consolation of Israel" (Lc 2:25), a promise of the Messiah.

4. In the NT the word appears 109 times with sense of to "invite" (Ac 28:20), "to ask" (Lc 7:4; Mt 8:5; Mr 5:12), "to beg" (Mt 25:53), "to exhort" (1 Co 14:3), "consol or encourage." Likewise in the NT, it is the principle function of the prophet (Ac 15:32; 16:40) and should be the ministry of every believer to each other (Phil 2:1). Timothy was sent to exhort the churches (1 Th 3:2). The instruction of how to exhort is "by our Lord Jesus Christ and by the love of the Spirit" (Rom 15:30) and "By the meekness and gentleness of Christ..." (2 Cor 10:1). It has always been necessary to warn people to continue faithful to the Lord (Acts 11:23), to continue in the faith (Ac 14:22) and to live with dignity (Eph 4:1). In the midst of heartache, loss and persecution the emphasis is the aspect of consolation (2 Co 1:3-4; 7:4; 1 Th 3:7; Rom 15:4; 2 Th 2:16).

B. Explanation

1. The gift can be manifested in various forms. Some will have the faith (confidence) to exhort, admonish and warn the whole congregation, motivating them to act Biblically. This could be in the form of preaching. Others will feel more comfortable exercising the gift in the ministry of counseling or leading a small group in applying the Bible to their lives.

2. It is the ability to come close to people causing them to feel uplifted, guided, helped, or corrected yet loved and accepted. It causes strengthening of the weak, consoling of the hurt and wounded, correcting those who have made mistakes and encouragement for those who are negative or disheartened.

3. The person with the gift has gained the respect of his peers because of his own application of the Scripture to his life. Those in the middle of problems and afflictions tend to listen with open hearts and minds to this person.

4. Shouting, showing anger, pointing a finger, or criticizing are not characteristic of this gift. Rather it shows compassion towards the unchurched, a sincere interest in others and the ability to correct behavior or communicate comfort and peace in the midst of their affliction.

5. Others seek those who have the gift of exhortation and ask for help or advice in solving their problems.

6. The gift can be exercised either in public or in private. There should be many in each church with this gift. They should not be afraid to use it.

7. The principle danger is pride, which can show itself as:
   a. Taking the credit for the results
   b Enjoying too much the sensation of popularity and importance
   c. Using other people to accomplish personal goals.
   d Abusing authority and demanding too much submission to solutions rendered, not giving
      room for others to decide between alternatives concerning their future.

C. Symptoms

1. Generally there is a strong reaction (in pro- or contra-) to the position or declarations presented
   by the exhorter. This gift expresses itself with much conviction.

2. Frequently this gifted person gives advice to others about how they should do things.

3. The exhorter delights in sharing the Word with others who are in need and loves knowing that
   they have been consoled. His motivation is to help others live biblically.

4. Others frequently confide in him their profound problems because they feel that he understands
   them.

5. Others could seek out his companionship because they feel secure, spiritual, stable and encouraged after being with him.

6. He is not satisfied with a superficial knowledge of the Truth, rather he looks for how the truths
   of Scriptures can be applied.

7. He likes to share aspects of his testimony with others because he knows that God will use it in
   their lives.

7. Word of wisdom

A. Definition

1. Study of the word and associated words

Greek	Etymology	Translation	Basic Idea	Passages
sophia		"wisdom, intelligence"	Intelligent application of truth	Acts 6:3, 10; 7:22; 1 Cor 1:19-20; Eph 1:8, 17; Jas 1:5; 3:13
sunesis	"union, send together"	"understanding, knowledge"	Quickness of comprehension	1 Cor 1:19; Eph 3:4; 2 Tim 2:7
noeo	"mind"	"understanding"	Direct one's mind; perceive, consider	Eph 3:4; Heb 11:3

2. In the Classical Greek, the noun *sophia* signified an attribute, not an activity (*sunesis* is "reason"). The term indicates a capacity and skillful knowledge (i.e. the *sophia* of a carpenter) especially applied to practical areas more than to theory. "Mastery of a skill is the primary meaning in Homer and for some time later. This is not just the skill itself, but mastery of it, and hence is an attribute of the gods and their gift to humanity...The first sages are wise in conduct as well as learning, and their learning embraces practical wisdom, e.g., in political judgment."

    Socrates' wisdom consists of the critical knowledge that autonomous wisdom is not wisdom at all. True wisdom knows being, but humans are not granted this knowledge. For Plato wisdom is acceptance of being. Ignorance brings us under the power of superstition. As the idea is divine, wisdom is proper only to God, but philosophy is possible in the power of gods, and through it one may attain to the four virtues, wisdom being the greatest of virtues. Aristotle equates wisdom and philosophy. Wisdom is attainable as the first and most complete form of knowledge, i.e., the knowledge of first causes. Wisdom is a theoretical virtue, not a practical one as in Plato. It contemplates the truth of first causes, not just what results from them. The sages or wise men were counselors to kings and governors.

3. In the OT (LXX) the term is used to translate the word, *hokmah*, "wise or wisdom" (Ex 28:3; 1 Kings 2:6; Psa 36:30; 89:12). "The translation "wise" or "wisdom" is inexact; it catches neither the range nor the precise meaning of the original languages, which suggest experienced and competent mastery of life and its various problems. The most common parallels have to do with perception, understanding, or skill, although parallels with uprightness and honesty are also common. The parallels show that action rather than thought is the point. In contrast, folly is a disorder that also finds expression in behavior." The concept is the major theme of Proverbs, a manual for attaining the attributes of God's wisdom for one's life.

    The term indicates a specialist's knowledge in a specific field like art (Ex 36:1), economics (Pr 8:18, 21), government (Pr 8:15), or education (1 Kings 5:9-14). It is the ability to dominate life (Pr 8:32-36). It is inseparable from the "fear of God" as a prime motivator for making correct decisions (Pr 1:7; 9:10; 15:33; Psa 111:10). God's ability to grant special wisdom when He desires is evident in the life of Solomon (1 Kings 3:5-14). His wisdom was manifested in just decisions (3:16-28).

4. In the NT the term is concentrated in 1 Cor 1-3 (25 times), where the special wisdom necessary to understand salvation comes only as a result of an intervention by the Spirit. All who know the truth of God's Word have the initial foundation of this wisdom (Eph 1:8) and are challenged to grow in its expansive richness (Col 1:10; 3:16; 4:5; Eph 5:15). It is linked with sunesis in Col 1:9 to combine the ideas of special knowledge for practical life (*sophia*) and the broader understanding of a world view (*sunesis*) that brings all of life into a comprehensive whole around the reality of God in Christ.

   James understood the wisdom of God in suffering (Jas 1:5) and the values of maturity that result. This trait becomes evident with the practical qualities of meekness, mildness, and a disciplined spirit (Jas 3:13, 17). Now the wisdom of God has been fully revealed in the Word so that we have all sufficiency for "everything we need for life and godliness" (2 Pet 1:3). It is chiefly a question of applying our hearts (desire) and minds (understanding through discipline) to learn and apply the wisdom that has been revealed.

5. There are some who want to understand the "word of wisdom" as a continual direct communication between God and the gifted person, in which divine truths, previously hidden are now revealed. Such revelations of the will of God were necessary in the years before the giving of the Spirit at Pentecost because all of the necessary wisdom of God had not been revealed. In those times, the acts of special communication from God were called sophia, "wisdom" in Rom 11:25-33; 1 Cor 2:6-7; Eph 3:1-10.

6. A distinction should be made between illumination and the revelation of wisdom. Practical wisdom is promised to every believer according to the measure of his understanding of the application of the Word already revealed (Eph 1:8; Col 1:9; James 1:5; 3:13, 17), while the Word of Wisdom is limited to a few in the church (1 Cor 12:14, 29-30). These gifted ones are to facilitate the understanding of the practical application of the wisdom of God in the lives of others. The gift is very similar to the gift of exhortation whose emphasis is more on the application, than the understanding of the wisdom.

B. Explanation

1. The connection between the "mystery" that was "hidden" (1 Cor 2:7) indicates that this wisdom was revealed by God directly, not indirectly through the Word already revealed. Peter made reference to the "wisdom" of Paul which was the basis of the revelation that he had received and later wrote by inspiration (2 Pet 3:15). This wisdom included the final destiny of Israel (Rom 11:25) and the participation by the Jews and Gentiles in one new Body (Eph 3:1-7).

2. It is the special ability to know how to apply the Word of God to the practical life in a given situation.

3. There are three aspects:
   a. Wisdom to respond to antagonistic courts (Mt 10:19-20): how to respond to accusations
   b. Wisdom to respond to arguments of unbelievers (1 Pet 3:15): how to defend yourself against skepticism, existentialism and irrationality.
   c. Wisdom to respond to difficult situations (James 1:5; 3:17): how to live in harmony with God's design for life.

4. The wisdom of God is available for all believers, but it must be sought and studied diligently, searching the Scriptures (Prov 2) with the conviction that it is worth the effort. Those who have made the effort find such practical wisdom for their lives that they become an invaluable resource for others. Those with the gift of Word of Wisdom will be able to explain and convince others to apply that wisdom to their lives.

C. Symptoms

1. There is an attraction for the study of the Bible, especially with the purpose of finding practical applications to the lives of individuals.

2. He senses frustration when sermons or Bible studies do not convey concrete applications to life's situations.

3. In any given life situation, specific principles or Biblical concepts of wisdom come to mind easily. He seems to be instrumental in finding solutions to personal and interpersonal conflicts (1 Cor 6:5). He is sought out for life's answers.

4. His vocational preference is to be a counselor (to impact individuals) or pastor-teacher (if his gift is to impact larger groups). God will create a desire in his heart to use the gift as He desires (Phil 3:12).

8. Word of knowledge

A. Definition

1. Study of the words

Greek	Etymology	Translation	Basic Idea	Passages
gnosis	*ginosko*- "to know"	"knowledge, understanding"	To perceive, recognize, comprehend, possession of information	1 Cor 8:1, 7; 12:8; Rom 15:14
gnosis		"acquaintance,	Means of knowing, thinking, judgment, opinion	Col 2:3; Acts 15:24; Luke 24:18

2. The original sense of the word found in the Classics was to know something personally, understand what others could not, and discern evidence that was not obvious. It implies a revelation so intimate that the concept of "knowing another" is used to refer to a sexual union. In fact, it is the root of the Latin word *gignere*, "to give birth." In the Hellenistic world, the Gnostics were those who supposedly had the knowledge of God and His will.

3. In the OT (LXX), *ginosko* was used to translate various concepts that the Jews saw as only one idea: *ra'ah*, "to see" (Jud 2:7), *hazah*, "see" (Isa 26:11) and *shama'*, "to hear" (Neh 4:15). Various words formed the root *yada*, "to know", which are translated by *gnoseos*. The word *yada* signifies (1) to experiment, to observe (Gen 3:7; 44441:31; Isa 47:8); (2) to know by learning (Prov 30:3); (3) an intimate relationship with other person or thing (Prov 2:6; Ecc 8:17); (4) to know the other person "face to face" (Deut 34:10; (5) the knowledge of God that is derived from the acts of self-revelation ("Know ye that I am God!" is mentioned 54 times in Ezekiel).

4. In the NT, *gnosis* appears 29 times (*ginosko*, 221 times). The concept of the OT is understood in the use of this word in the NT, especially because the LXX was practically the OT Bible in the times of Jesus. There is a sense that all the believers have received the "knowledge" of God, as is declared in 2 Cor 4:6. The knowledge of God is our experience, because God reveals Himself to the believer. Thus the gift of knowledge is the result of an illumination, on God's part through His Word. It appears that the knowledge of the will of God is similar to the gift of prophecy.

5. The gift is the capacity to understand, organize and clearly illuminate the thoughts of God, which are impossible to describe or know by mere human reasoning.

6. In 1 Cor 13:2, the gifts of prophecy and "Word of knowledge" are related. They are related to revealing "mysteries", the previously unknowable information that God chose to reveal through these gifted people. It is closely associated in this function with the gift of apostleship, or at best, indicates a very high level of authority in the revelation of God's will.

7. In a general sense, every believer is obligated to grow in the knowledge of the Scriptures already revealed (2 Pet 3:18). This growth will result from a diligent study, whereas before the written Word was complete, a special revelation was necessary. When one commits himself to study with the intention of obeying what is understood and already revealed, the Spirit is responsible to illuminate our mind with the riches of His Word (Jn 7:17).

B. Explanation

1. Knowledge, as a gift, is useful when it is communicated. It seems to be a gift related to the gift of teaching, but has more authority, that is, the teacher will cite the understanding of the gift of knowledge.

2. In the beginning of the church age it was probably a means of communicating the new revelation of the Word until its completion. If it is applicable today, it is the gift of the understanding of what has previously been revealed. This understanding is also supernatural (1 Cor 2:7-16), but it is not in the sense of being a new revelation.

3. Today, scholars dedicate their lives to the study of the knowledge recorded in the Scriptures in the original languages, the apparent problems and the defense of the faith.

4. In 1 Cor 13:8, there is a categorical statement that "knowledge will cease." God said that He would not continue to reveal new knowledge once all the necessary knowledge had been revealed. In Hebrews 1:1 the author stated that "in the past God spoke to our forefathers through the prophets at many times and in various ways", but that age came to a close with Jesus and His apostles, who became the only source of the revelation of God's knowledge. The gift of knowledge by revelation ended, but God continued to illuminate His Word to men dedicated to investigate the record of all God has revealed.

5. It could be that the "revelation" of 1 Cor 14:26 that could be declared in the congregation came by the gift of knowledge (?).

6. The gift of knowledge is associated with the gifts of tongues and prophecy in 1 Cor 13:8, where all three are declared to be temporary by the apostle Paul. During the period of the revelation of the Word of God, which came "in parts" (13:9) to those having the gifts of prophecy and knowledge. These gifted people had key roles in putting into our hands all that God wanted the Church to know for all the Church Age. The gifts of exhorting and teaching would continue the applications of all that prophecies and the revelations of knowledge gave to the vast reservoir of wisdom and understanding for the church.

9. Helps, service

A. Definition:

1. Study of the word and associated words

Greek	Etymology	Translation	Basic Idea	Passages
antilepsis	anti- "in exchange -lambano, "take, laying hold of"	help, aid	Taking charge to help	1 Cor 12:28 (only use)
diakonia	"service"	ministry, service, deacon	Basic nuance of personal service. Willingness to sacrifice yourself in practical service for others.	Rom 12:7; 15:31; 1 Cor 16:15
sunergos	sun- "with" -ergos, "labor"	collaborator	A helper in the labor	1 Cor 16:16; 2 Tim 4:17; Rom 16:2
douleuo	doulos, "slave;" "be subjected"	serve	Obey your commander; serve as a slave your master	Acts 20:19; Ro 12:11;14:18; Eph 6:7; Col 3:24

2. This gifted person is willing to involve himself in the needs of others to help them, or to assist others in the ministry. It is used especially to help the weak and needy (1 Th 5:14).

3. The gift of helps is manifested by the ability to satisfy the needs of others, not from any egotism or personal benefit, rather from the desire to offer practical helps to those in need. The type of work necessary ican be multiple and varied.

4. The gift is called "helps" in 1 Cor 12:28; "service" in Rom 12:7. All the gifts are "services" or "ministries" (diakonia), but this gift functions in a practical or facilitator role making possible the normalcy of life or the functioning of another ministry. The example is given in Acts 6:1-3 where the "service" to the apostles alleviated their burdensome responsibilities so they could fulfill their priority ministries.

5. Examples of this gift are Epaphroditus (Phil 2:25-30), Onesiphrous (2 Ti 1:16-18); Onesimous (Philemon 10-13).

B. Explanation

1. The gift of helps functions to provide practical services in the church ministry and to help the needy members of the church (Ac 20:35; 1 Cor 16:15-16).

2. A person with this gift does not need or seek fame, nor does he need to be recognized publicly, but is absolutely indispensable to the ministry of the church.

3. It is one who occupies himself arranging, cleaning, repairing, preparing meals or in whatever activity necessary for the on-going of the ministry. He makes sure that the spoken ministry is

successful.

4. The "service" may be in a spiritual form (in 2 Cor 1:11, "as you help us by your prayers...") or a practical form (Rom 16:9; Phil 4:3), so long as the overall ministry prospers and is unhindered by distracting problems that someone can resolve.

5. Probably hospitality (1 Ti 3:2; Tit 1:8; 1 Pet 4:9) is one aspect of the gift of helps (Rom 12:13; Heb 13:1), which is to be practiced by all who can. This is a requirement for a leadership role, "hospitable" (1 Tim 3:2).

6. The manifestation of "helps" is related directly to expressions of love (1 Cor 12:31-13:13). The nature of the gift does not naturally receive much or any public recognition as other gifts might. Thus it is only when love is abounding as the continual motivation with the gift of helps that it proves to be beneficial to the church body.

7. As with many of the gifts, the responsibility to "help one another" is the responsibility of everyone. Those that have the gift of service/helps should not be the only ones involved in helping others, but their example and collaboration should teach everyone how to serve.

8. Studies of thousands of churches have revealed that approximately 70% of the church body will manifest the gift of helps/service. Its importance cannot be overestimated.

C. Symptoms

1. A person with this gift will recognize and be sensitive to the needs that people and organizations have, while finding within a desire to help others in any form or any need.

2. The ability to see many ways to help others, spiritual, temporal or physical. It provides practical service to another as opposed to informational or psychological help.

3. An unselfish nature that finds great personal satisfaction in doing what others can not do for themselves or do not have time, resources or experience to do in order to help meet a need.

4. Normally God has providentially given previous training or skills that bring personal satisfaction in exercising their skill. The object is to bring about the success of a project or program. The satisfaction of a job well done is sufficient motivation to keep this person giving of him/herself.

5. The recognition that leadership or speaking gifts may not be his area of expertise, yet there is a strong desire to be a team player to facilitate the different ministries in the church. There is a willingness to do whatever it takes to bring about the success of an overall ministry. The spiritual gift gives special grace to keep on giving to needs without the need of recognition or receiving appreciation. This is an indispensable gift for the church.

10. Giving

A. Definition:

1. Study of the word and words associated

Greek	Etymology	Translation	Basic Idea	Passages
metadidomi	*meta-* "with" -*didomi*, "give"	"give, share equally"	Giving to meet the needs of others or ministries	Rom 1:11; 12:8; Eph 4:28
dorea	*doron-* "gift"	"free, gift, without pay"	Gift that has been given, sometimes in legal sense	Acts 11:17; Rom 3:24; Eph 3:7
apodidomi	*apo-* "back" -*didomi*, "give"	"restore, return"	To give with the idea of a return	Matt 5:26; 1 Tim 5:4; 2 Tim 4:8; Heb 13:17

2. In the Classics the word *metadidomi* had the idea of sharing to meet the needs of others; to personally feel the needs of the poor. The word *doreomai* emphasized the grace of receiving something that is not deserved.

3. In the OT (LXX) *didomi* is used to translate the Hebrew word *natan*, "to give": (1) to other men (Prov 4:2); (2) of men giving to God (Lev 7:15); (3) of God giving to men (Gen 30:20).

4. In the NT, the word *didomi* is used 416 times. The chief example in the NT is of God Himself (Jn 4:10; Gal 1:4; 1 Tim 2:6). The response of the believer should be to give to God following the example that God has already set (Rom 12:1; 2 Cor 8:5). Once a person has willingly given to God all he is or has, he begins to act as a steward of God's possessions (that he had previously given back to God) and now are seen as being entrusted to his care. He distributes as God would indicate by providence (providentially being in the presence of need) or by participation, seeking to facilitate the advancement of the kingdom through partnering with laborers (Phil 4:17-19).

5. The key descriptive word that should control the act of giving is "simplicity" (Rom 12:8). It is the word *aplotes*, meaning singleness of purpose, mentally honest. It is one free from pretense and hypocrisy, not self seeking or wanting anything in return, rather only wanting to be generous, which is the true symptom of the gift of giving.

B. Explanation

1. The one who possesses the gift of giving has the ability to give of his personal possessions for needy people (especially in the church) and for the advancement of the kingdom through the local church ministry. This giving is consistent, self-motivated, with a sense of joyous sacrifice and such delight in giving that the attitude becomes contagious throughout the church.

2. According to 2 Cor 8:2, the gift of giving is not limited to the rich.

3. As in the OT, the giving included much more than the tithe. The OT follower actually had three tithes in the law (though one was only given every 3 years so it amounted to 3.3% per year) thus amounting to a total of 23% per year had to be set aside for the Lord.

4. The tithe is an OT concept and did not originate in a law concept since it was practiced 600

years before the law (Gen 14:20). The references in the NT are scarce, probably because it was an assumed principle carried over from the Jewish heritage. In Mt 23:23 Jesus criticized the Pharisees for making a show of their tithing, while not fulfilling the rest of the law regarding "justice, mercy and faithfulness". Jesus declares that true believers will practice both tithing and justice.

5. A somewhat more remote connection to the OT tithe in the NT is in 1 Cor 9:13, where Paul is laying the foundations for NT giving in the church, especially in regard to the supporting of full-time pastors. The comparison is made just as in the OT the giving of a tithe to the Temple was to support the priestly leadership, so in the NT the giving (of a tithe?) would support the pastoral staff.

6. The gift is particularly evident in the ability to be generous with delight beyond the normal level of giving. Numerous people have been able to give 30-50% of their income, while some wealthier have attained the giving level of 80-90% of their income to the Lord's work (2 Cor 9:7).

7. This is one of the gifts that is necessary to cultivate and brings one to maturity. It is not natural or necessarily easy, but the grace of this gift permits a generous spirit that becomes an example to the whole church. The two-fold motivation in this giving is (1) to transfer as much "treasure" (Mt 6:19-21) to a heavenly account (Phil 4:17), revealing that his heart is really set on the kingdom, and (2) to trust God for a supernatural and providential reimbursement so as to repeat the cycle of being able to give more (Phil 4:19). In that verse (4:19) the need that God has promised to supply is the need that resulted from having been so generous to the ministry of Paul that the givers were in need or impoverished.

8. Anything given in the name of the Lord and for His purpose in the world will not lack its recompense (Mt 10:41-42), thus its uses are three-fold:
   a. Meet the need of other members of the church (Eph 4:28; Gal 6:10)
   b. Meet the needs of other churches (2 Cor 8-9; Rom 15:25-26)
   c. Meet the needs of their full time spiritual leadership (Phil 4:10; Gal 6:9; 1 Cor 9:1-11; 1 Tim 6:16)

C. Symptoms

1. A sensitivity to recognize the physical and material needs of others.

2. A quickness and creativity to assume the burden to help others.

3. A profound conviction that all our possessions belong to God and that Christians are stewards given the responsibility to distribute the wealth, skills or resources that God has put in their trust.

4. The ability to make finances grow in order to use them for God, with the purpose of increasing the distribution of God's funds.

5. The ability to carefully manage finances with the tendency to retain only what is necessary, in order to maximize the giving potential.

6. His delight and joy in life is sharing with others and seeing that his provision was just what a brother or ministry needed, or was instrumental in advancing the gospel.

11. Govern, lead, administrate

A. Definitions

1. Study of the words associated with this gift:

Greek	Etymology	Translation	Basic Idea	Passages
kuberngsis	*kubernao-* "act of steering a ship"	"steer, guide or govern"	The skill with which a pilot guides a ship, administrative ability.	1 Cor 12:28
kubernetes	"steersman"	"helmsman, pilot, statesman; captain of a ship"	The one who has authority and direction of a ship or an organization	Acts 27:11; Rev 18:17
proistemi	*pro-* "before" *-istemi*, "stand"	"preside, lead, be in charge."	The leader that others want to follow toward a goal; a visionary.	Rom 12:8; 1 Thes 5:12; 1 Tim 3:4, 5; 5:17
hegeomai	"go before; rule; command"	"govern, lead, be the boss, judge, or pastor"	The one who has authority and makes decisions for others.	Matt 2:6; Acts 7:10; 15:22; Heb 13:7, 17, 24

2. In the OT (LXX), *kubernesis* is used in relation with wisdom. In Proverbs 12:5 it is translated "counsels." In Ezekiel 27:8 it is used for the word "pilots."

3. The Greek word, *kubernetes*, is the origin of the word "cybernetics" or the science of the relationship between the brain and the control of the body. It is necessary that this gift be recognized in the leadership of a church (*proistemi* for "govern" in 1 Tim 5:17). It is the ability to make decisions, be responsible for the actions of others and to take initiatives. Though these three gifts are taken together, they may refer to different functions or gifted ministries.

4. It is the pilot of the ship that makes the decisions for the direction and has the responsibility for the route to be taken for arriving at a port (Ac 27:11); thus it refers to someone who must maintain the biblical direction of the church as a captain of a ship. Obviously it implies that he has been granted the authority to determine the direction.

5. It is the ability to organize and administrate with such efficiency and selflessness that the project is completed satisfactorily while maintaining harmony and motivation within the group.

6. The gifts of "ruling" (Rom 12:8) and "administration" (1 Cor 12:28) are similar enough to be treated together, though they may be as different as "leader" and "manager."

B. Explanation

1. What it is not: the natural tendency to dominate a situation or persons in order to attain the leader's goals. The gift of the Spirit never is a demagoguery, or a dictatorship (1 Pet 5:3). This type of leadership is prohibited in Mark 10:42-44. The testimony of Diotrephes (3 John) is the result of having

permitted a dogmatic leader to dominate a church.

2. Christian leadership is expressed in wisdom, spiritual example, and humility, meeting the needs of those under his authority, he is to be respected personally. This is the reason to esteem and respect pastors in 1 Th 5:12-13. It is not just for the office of pastor, but for his character and service to others. Leadership is the ability to recognize the gifts and ministries of others, equip and organize them efficiently to eliminate the doubling of efforts and the confusion that results when people are not prepared for their responsibilities. A leader takes maximum advantage of the strengths of each member with the objective of reaching the purposes that God desires of the ministry.

3. The gift could lead to a full-time ministry opportunity in a local church. The character requirements of leadership (1 Tim 3:1-7; Titus 1:5-9) would be necessary to assume such a position. As a man "governs" his family, he will also "govern" the church (1 Tim 3:4-5). The first place to make evident the gift of administration or leadership is within the family unit. If this person is not able to resolve problems within the family and lead them to be obedient, he will not be able to do so in the church. The requirement seems to imply that the authority given to this gifted person will compare to the father in a family.

4. Paul insisted that all the activities and functions of the church are to be done decently and in order (1 Cor 14:33, 40). The gift that best assures this goal is the use of the gift of administration. It is a great benefit that someone in the leadership of the church or organization have the gift of administration or know how to govern well (1 Tim 5:17). This will allow other pastor(s)/elders to be able to dedicate themselves to the study, prayer and teaching of the Word.

5. Some suggestions derived from 1 Cor 12:28:
   a) The gift has less authority than an apostle, prophet or teacher.
   b) Although it may receive recognition, it is not equal to the speaking or sign gifts.
   c) Since a lot of the labor is not before the public, but behind the scenes, it is a labor of love, as a gift of help.
   d) Continue organizing programs even though there may not be an expressed appreciation for their contribution, will require a high level of devotion to the Lord and to the members of the body.
   e) Through the power of the spiritual gift the administrator will continue on even with hurt feelings from other leaders or misunderstandings.

C. Symptoms

1. This person has a tendency to organize people and things with ease.
2. He/She feels uncomfortable when an organization or program doesn't function perfectly, or when a leader does not delegate authority or doesn't explain all the aspects of a project for the completion or strategic partner.
3. This person likes to invent methods or infra-structures for all organizations.
4. He thinks in terms of how to help others reach their goals.
5. He likes to do things to help others to be more efficient.
6. It is not a difficulty for this person to assume responsibilities and take charge of details even when the plans need to be changed.

12. Mercy

A. Definition:

1. Study of the words

Greek	Etymology	Translation	Basic Ideas	Passages
eleos	"compassion, pity"	"show mercy, pity, compassion"	A motive of pity upon seeing someone afflicted.	Rom 12:8; Matt 5:7; 1 Tim 1:13
eleemosune	*ele-* "mercy"	"sympathy, donations, charity"	An act of goodness motivated by compassion	Matt 6:1-4; Acts 9:36

2. The gift refers to the ability to feel compassion for those that are in need, especially for those who do not merit help or those who nobody is interested in helping, etc. He shows this compassion in practical forms with an attitude of joy that encourages those in need (Ac 9:36). It is an uncritical attitude toward the undeserving or helpless.

3. In the Classics, *eleos* is an emotion produced upon making contact with an afflicted person who does not deserve affection. It is the opposite of the feeling of envy for the good fortune of another. It is a feeling of pity for the less fortunate.

4. In the OT (LXX) the word is used 400 times, mainly to translate *hased*, "loyal love." The concept changes from the relation in the Classics. Now it is more a judicial or legal sense. Hased is a behavior based on a commitment or covenant. It is the responsibility or loyalty from one person to another to demonstrate kindness, pity or grace.

5. In the NT *eleos* is used 78 times. In the gospels the needy cried for "mercy," asking for healing from Jesus (Mr 10:47, 48). The mercy of man towards man (Mt 5:7; 18:33) is imitated from the mercy of God towards man. The mercy of salvation by grace is a motive to act similarly (Eph 2:4-10; 2 Cor 4:1; Rom 12:1; Jas 3:17).

B. Explanation

1. The gift of mercy is manifested in compassion, understanding, patience and feeling towards the needy or hurting.

2. The gift of mercy motivates a joyous and voluntary giving of one's self, of your time, your privacy, your resources, etc. in order to benefit the needy. The recompense is a satisfaction that is hard to explain.

3. There are three descriptive aspects of the gift of mercy:
   a. Feeling of compassion
   b. Motivation to an act of help or assistance and motivate others to help.
   c. Sense of joy and satisfaction.

4. Mercy should be an expression of kindness or goodness in all believers (fruit of the Spirit), but the gift of mercy is the area of lifetime dedication. The fruit of the Spirit shows mercy when the opportunity presents itself, but the gift of mercy looks for the opportunity to structure a permanent and practical long term solutions for the needy to demonstrate the mercy of Christ for the needy.

5. The gift has special evangelistic applications for the preparation of the hearts of the unconverted creating a willingness to listen to the gospel message even in hostile environments.

6. It is the response of the church to the problems of society. It can be the testimony most recognized in the world to demonstrate the faith in Christ in a concrete form.

7. This gift is directed towards those experiencing hurt, rejection, depression, loss, poverty, lack of love, physical affliction, starvation, addiction (drugs or alcohol) or similar desperate needs.

C. Symptoms

1. This person reacts emotionally on hearing or seeing sad circumstances. He is easily involved emotionally in circumstances of others.

2. Other people remark that this person has a personality that feels the emotions of others.

3. He/she expresses a desire to reach and help those who are living in misery or overwhelming circumstances, habits or hurting situations.

4. He feels empathy for the wounds of others.

5. He desires to express love (or the love of Christ) to the desperate and destitute.

6. Those in need like to have this person in their presence because he/she makes them glad and gives them hope.

7. He never feels rejection or repulsion toward the poor, sick or hurting, rather thinks, "How can I help?"

8. Often this person has needed mercy and it changed his life, so they want to help others as they were given mercy.

13. Faith

A. Definition:

1. Study of the word and associated words

Greek	Etymology	Translation	Basic Idea	Passages
pistis	*pist-* "trust"	"faith"	Trust in someone or thing	1 Cor 12:9; 13:2
apistis	*a-* "without" *-pist-* "trust"	"unbeliever"	Does not trust in anything.	Matt 17:17; Rev 20:8
peitho	*peit-* "trust" (same root word as *pistos*)	"convince, persuade"	Trust in something	Matt 27:20, 43; Mark 10:24; Heb 13:17
peitharcheo	*peit-* "trust" *-archeo,* "rule"	"obey a ruler or superior"	Trust controls your actions in obedience	Acts 5:29; Titus 3:1
apeithes	*a-* "no, without" *-peit-,* "trust"	"disobey"	Lack of trust results in a refusal to obey.	Rom 11:32; Heb 4:6

2. In the Classics, *pisteuo* signified confidence or trust in someone or something. As a noun, *pistos*, it meant the faithfulness of people tied by a covenant. *Pistis* implies a certainty, trust and assurance for the completion of a promise. The word is tightly associated with obedience, i.e. a trustworthy person is going to fulfill whatever is his assignment.

3. In the OT (LXX) the concept of "faith" translates the word '*aman*, "be faithful, truthful, and trust-worthy." It is confidence in an unalterable and undoubted act such that all the coming generations will have to accept (Isa 7:9). In Hebrew there is no word for "persuade or convince." Another root word to *pistos* is *peitho*, "obedient", but it is not used in the LXX, however, the negation *apeitheo*, "disobedient" is used frequently (Dt 1:26; Isa 3:8). Thus the concept of a person of faith refers to an obedient person who believes God means what He says. Faith and fear are closely related in the OT; although contradictory, they shade into one another, and together they express the living tension and polar dynamic of the OT relationship to God. They occur more or less equally.

4. In the NT, *pistis* demands a full absolute trust in what Christ promised, but some were also going to receive the gift of faith (1 Cor 12:9) in addition to the saving faith. An exaggeration of this gift is referred to in the phrase "have all faith" (1 Cor 13:2), which is part of a series of exaggerations or hyperboles of certain gifts that are valueless without a loving commitment to use one's gifts for the benefit of others. However, this would imply a variety of possible levels of faith.

This gift should be distinguished from the Word of knowledge and Word of wisdom, which may have been instruments for delivering the inspired Word, while the gift of faith declares what God is going to do in a particular circumstance. It implies much conviction about what God is going to do and a sure confidence that He will do it.

B. Explanation

1. It is necessary to distinguish among four types of faith in the NT:
   a. *Saving faith*: placing one's trust, once and for all, in the redeeming work of Christ for our salvation and acceptance before God (Eph 2:8). This faith is not limited, rather is universal among all

believers.

b. *Doctrinal faith* is a composite of biblical doctrines (Ac 14:22; 16:5; Rom 1:5)

c. *Fruit of faith* is one of the nine aspects of the fruit of the Spirit (Gal 5:22). This faith is not limited to a few, rather should be universal to all believers, especially those filled with the Spirit.

d. *Spiritual gift of faith* is a special limited gift of the Spirit for some believers in the body, but not for all (1 Cor 12:11, 18), given primarily to minister to and encourage others, building up their faith, so they will trust God and act by faith in difficult and impossible situations.

2. The gift of faith is a manifestation of an intense trust in God with which God gives the ability for some to trust in the power of God to conquer enormous obstacles or impossibilities. Paul made a reference to an exaggerated gift of faith in 1 Cor 13:2, "if I had all faith that can move mountains, but have not love, I am nothing." Even if one had this authority, if exercised without benefiting others he would be useless for the kingdom, if not harmful. This is a reference to the teaching of Jesus in Mt 17:20 where He promised special powers to his disciples immediately after casting out a demon from a child.

3. The experience of the apostles seemed to join the gift of faith to the gift of prophecy. In Ac 27:25 Paul was told by prophecy that certain events would take place, then he announced it by faith with the results that it happened "as he had said" (Ac 27:44).

4. Three aspects of the gift of faith:

a. An extraordinary or intuitive understanding of the will of God in specific situations (1 Jn 5:14-15; Mt 17:20-21).

b. The gift tends to specialize in the impossible, humanly speaking (2 Cor 16:9), perhaps because it will be more evident that only God could make it happen precisely, such that He is honored.

c. The announcement of what will happen in the future for the glory of God.

5. Abraham is an example (Rom 4:20). God told him a promise of what He was going to do. For years Abraham remained faithful to the promise that God had given and finally received the announced promise. The gift of faith is basically obedience to the promises that God has given applying them to specific situations where God will fulfill His purpose.

6. Paul had a vision of what God was going to do and he followed that vision all of his life (Ac 9:15; 26:16-20). God gives a leader a vision through faith, if he is willing to pay the price of pursuing it over the years, He will bring it to pass. Great leaders have manifested incredible faith launching out to accomplish the impossible.

7. God uses the gift of faith:

a. To bring glory to Himself, that is, to reveal Himself in real life's situations such that it is unmistakably God who did it..

b. To exhort the church to pray and believe in a God who responds to our prayers.

c. To meet the needs of the church and individuals through answered prayer.

C. Symptoms

1. This person desires to accept the Biblical promises in the literal sense and apply them to specific situations until God meets the need. As an evangelist manifests his gift to facilitate the winning of souls, the one who has the gift of faith manifests his ability to see answers to his prayers.

2. A special ability to understand what God is going to do in a situation through a clear understanding of the application of His promises and a disposition to wait in confidence until God responds.

3. In some circumstances he has the sense that God is working, even when others have lost hope.

4. With the repetition of successful experiences of answered prayer, the confidence that God is going to respond again mounts higher, not only in the life of the gifted one, but also in those who know him and observe his answers to prayer. This results in a contagious growth of trust in God's ability to intervene in one's daily life.

5. He has a strong desire to know God in His fullness and depend on Him completely for the solutions of difficult circumstances. Eventually the boldness of attempting the impossible becomes almost natural. These experiences show that God is alive and powerful today. He responds to our prayers without any manipulation of men or negotiating with men (i.e., "If you do this, then I will …").

6. This special confidence in Him, not only believes that God "can" do it, but that He "will" do it or "already has" done what was asked.

14. Discernment of spirits

A. Definitions

1. Study of the word

Greek	Etymology	Translation	Basic Idea	Passages
diakrisis	*dia-* for emphasis *-krino*, "distinguish, judge"	"separate, judge, distinguish, discern"	Ability to mark a difference between the true and false.	Rom 14:1; 1 Cor 12:10; Heb 5:14
diakrino verb form	As above	"decide, judge, distinguish"	Examine, search, assess, evaluate	1 Cor 11:29; 14:29; 6:5

2. In the Classics, the word signified the ability to arrange things by categories, to make decisions or judge between alternatives for judgments or justice.

3. In the OT (LXX) the term translates the Hebrew word *sapat* (Ex 18:16; 1 Kings 3:9; Prov 31:9) that means "examine or search something to decide."

4. In the NT the word is used 16 times to refer to judging signs (Mt 16:3), judging one's self (1 Cor 11:31), and the words of prophets in the church (1 Cor 14:29). This word has such varied meanings as "separation," "distinction," "strife," "appraisal," and "exposition." In the NT it usually means "discernment" or "differentiation" (between spirits in 1 Cor. 12:10, between good and evil in Heb. 5:14). Instead of appealing to the courts of law, the believers are exhorted to depend upon men of discernment in the church relations (1 Cor 6:5) to decide what is right when there are disputes. There are similar uses in Ac 11:2 and Judas 9.

5. It is the ability to determine if a teacher, preacher, exhorter or pastor is speaking under the direction of the Holy Spirit, his own spirit or evil spirits (2 Cor 11:14-15).

6. It is the capacity to distinguish between truth and error, comparing the evidence with the Truth revealed or principles of the truth. It is the ability to distinguish false doctrine from true, though we are all called upon to make these judgment calls. This person intuitively knows the source of teachings.

7. The discernment is of "spirits". It is the same original word mentioned in 1 Cor 14:12, where it is translated "spiritual gifts" or "manifestations of the Spirit". Thus it is a discernment between which spirit is motivating the words or actions.

B. Explanation

1. In the Early Church there were prophets, itinerate teachers, those claiming to be apostles, evangelists, and preachers going from church to church. Without a written NT for the first 25-35 years of the church age, there was an early dependency upon the gift of discernment in the local church. They practiced discernment or judgment frequently (2 Cor 11:13; 2 Pet 2:1; Rev 2:2, 14, 20).

2. The church, with the written Bible, still needs discernment to protect itself from the errors of the natural tendency towards myths, error, exaggerations, legends, traditions, fables, heresies and bad practices (1 Jn 4:1-3) that so easily slip into the church belief structure just as it did in the Early Church. The gift of discernment has the exceptional ability to sense error in the making.

3. There are three areas of evaluation where the gift of discernment operates today:
    a) Discern the quality, sincerity and genuineness of a teacher or preacher (1 Cor 14:29)
    b) Discern the words of a preacher in order to evaluate his teaching in light of the written Word (Acts 17:11).
    c) Discern the best decision or judgment in conflicts and disputes between brethren (1 Cor 6:1-8).

4. Paul warned that in the last days there would be an increase in false teachers (1 Tim 4:1), so this gift is even more necessary as we enter the "last days" before Jesus comes.

5. Special warnings concerning those who speak of doctrines recently revealed by angels or false prophets. Note that in 1 Thes 5:21 it is the responsibility of everyone not to be deceived.

6. There should always be a discerning spirit in the church (1 Cor 14:29).

7. An example of discernment is in Ac 16:17. "These men are servants of the Most High God, who are telling you the way to be saved." However, Paul had the discernment to recognize this declaration as a demonic origin and rebuked it (16:16, 18), even though what was said was correct.

C. Symptoms

1. He has the ability to recognize the inconsistencies in persons and teachings, without being unnecessarily critical.
2. He always wants to examine what is taught or preached for what might be an error or could be improved.
3. He possesses the ability to categorize teachings and recognize the source of different teachings.
4. This person thinks in logical steps, recognizing tendencies in teachings and emphasis.
5. He has a good understanding of the Scriptures. (The best way to recognize a counterfeit bill is to have memorized the characteristics of a genuine bill).
6. He easily recognizes bad interpretations or applications in lessons and sermons.
7. He senses an uneasiness that will not let him accept a situation on hearing only half of the truth or when the truth is wrongly applied or even when false teaching is accepted by everyone else.

15. Miracles

A. Definitions

1. Study of the associated words

Greek	Etymology	Translation	Basic Idea	Passages
dunameis	*duna-* "power, force"	"miracle, power, force, authority"	able to produce a strong power, inherent ability.	1 Cor 12:10; 12:29; Acts 9:40; 8:13; 19:11
semeion	*sema-* "mark, indicator"	"sign, miracle, marvel"	An indicator of what God wants to communicate; authentication.	Heb 2:4; 2 Cor 12:12; 2 Thes 3:17; Matt 16:3
energia	"action, operation"	"power, energy"	Working, power in exercise, operative power.	Eph 1:19; 3:7; 4:16; Col 1:29; 2:12; Phil 3:21
exousia	"power, authority to do a thing"	"authority"	Liberty of action, right, authority, delegated power.	John 5:27; 2 Cor 10:8; 1 Tim 2:12; Titus 2:15
ischuo	"be strong, healthy"	"able, strength"	Be sound, able to do something, wield power.	James 5:16; Matt 5:13; Gal 5:6, 13; Phil 4:13
kratos	"sovereign power"	"power devoted to control, supremacy"	Might, relative and manifested power, chiefly used of God.	Eph 1:19; 6:12; 1 Pet 4:11; 5:11

2. The gift of miracles includes much more than the gift of healings. It could be related to the gift of faith, that is, an opportune miracle or other signs could manifest the gift of faith. An example of a miracle is the resurrection of someone that recently died (Ac 9:40) or when Elymus,- the sorcerer, was left blind by Paul (Ac 13:8-11). The consequence of the events in Acts 13 was that everyone was intent on what Paul wanted to say.

3. In the Classics, the word *dunamis* was used to refer to the power or authority of a governor or a king. It would be a military or political power. The *dunamis* of nature (storms, winds, etc) were considered a manifestation of the power of the gods. Through magic invented by man, one could share or obtain such powers. "The fundamental concept in the Greek sphere, then, is that of a natural force which, imparted in different ways, controls, moves, and governs the cosmos."

4. In the OT (LXX) *dunamis* is used to translate *hayil* (military force). The word *dunamis* should be distinguished from *ischys*, which signifies a physical force or power. *Dunamis* tended to emphasize more the authority over something in stead of a physical force. Thus it is the right to have something supernatural. "The decisive difference in the OT is that the power of a personal God replaces the neutral force of nature that is equated with deity."

5. In the NT *dunamis* is used 118 times. It is a demonstration of the power of God over nature, life, death and, especially, over other spirit beings. There are other "powers" between heaven and earth that can manifest themselves in people (Mr 13:25; Rom 8:38; Eph 1:21; 1 Pet 3:22). The power of these supernatural beings was broken and soon will be destroyed completely (Mt 12:29; Lk 11:22; 10:19; 1 Cor 15:24; 2 Thes 2:9; Rev 13:2; 17:13). The majority of the manifestations of *dunamis* are

in direct confrontation with these satanic powers (Mt 12:22-30; Mr 6:2, 5; Lk 19:37).

B. Explanation

1. There are three words primarily associated with "miracles" in the NT:
   a) "Power": an event of an obvious supernatural power (9 times translated "miracle").
   b) "Marvel": an event that astounds people (16 times is translated "miracle") as something naturally impossible, not even by coincidence.
   c) "Sign": an event that indicates something significant or divine (60-70 times that it occurs is translated "miracle"), because its nature is so divine it authenticates a speaker or his message as being from God.

2. There are three aspects of the gift of miracles:
   a) A supernatural event, something that goes against the laws of nature, something that is impossible to explain by any coincidence. They were manifested in the Bible as:
      (1) Power over sicknesses (related to the gift of immediate and visible healings)
      (2) Power over nature (related to calming the storm, walking on water, iron axes floating, etc.)
      (3) Power over matter (related to changing water to wine, multiplying the fish and bread)
   b) An event that can be perceived by the senses: to "marvel" means "to look at the details." It is an immediate visible change that is irrefutable.
   c) An event that accompanies a servant of God to authenticate his position and authority: a sign.
      1) Occurs every time there is a new revelation from God. He sends the power and authority to do miracles in order to confirm his messengers (John 6:14; 2 Cor 12:12; Rom 15:18-19; Mr 16:20; Heb 2:3-4)
      2) Once His new revelation and His messenger were accepted or authenticated, the power to continue to do miracles ceased (i.e., the burning bush, staff turning to a snake and back to a staff, etc.). Believers are expected to accept the miraculous evidence once delivered and confirmed by witnesses as sufficient for faith. There is no need for repetition, but faith can trust the evidence of apostolic signs.

3. Why were miracles abundant in the apostolic age and almost immediately thereafter ceased?
   a) Was it for the unbelief of the early believers?
      1) This position would condemn to unbelief hundreds of thousands of men of faith and the power of the Spirit throughout Church History who never saw or could do a miracle.
      2) Could it be possible for someone to manifest the fruit of the Spirit and the power to edify the church, yet still have an unbelieving heart? (Heb 3:12)
   b) Was it the will of God for such miracles to cease or rarely to occur?

4. Do you know someone who has the power to suspend the laws of nature by his own will like Moses? Elijah? Or Paul?

5. It appears that in the NT only Jesus, the apostles and a few people who had received the imposition of hands of an apostle, had this power to perform miracles (Compare Mark 16:16-20 with Heb 2:3-4).

6. Today many are seeking a sign or a miracle to verify their belief. In Jn 4:48 (Luke 11:29) but this attitude does not please God. Look at Luke 1:18-20. Why did Zacharias remain mute until the birth of John?

7. The miracles, in a broad sense, do occur occasionally today. They occur as miraculous answers to prayer: precise financial support at the exact time needed or a special protection in an accident, etc. Some would make a distinction of this type of miracle as a "providential" intervention of God

using natural means to meet special needs. These "miracles" usually don't result in a ceasing of the natural law, as an iron axe floating on command (2 Kings 6:5-6), but their coincidence and timing or precise answer to prayer to solve impossible or improbably situations that could be no accident, but rather God's intervention.

8. There was no developing or maturing of this gift: either you had it and could change the laws of nature or you couldn't.

9. It is better seen as a confirming gift that was temporary to the Early Church (as history makes evident) as part of God's plan as were other sign gifts, as indicated by Heb 2:3-4.

16. Healing

A. Definitions

1. Study of the associated words

Greek	Etymology	Translation	Basic Idea	Passages
iama	iama- "cure"	"heal, remedy, medicine"	Ability to cause people to be well.	1 Cor 12:9, 28, 30; John 12:40; Acts 10:38; 28:27
therapeia	"serve, care for, attend, treat"	"serve, heal worship"	Treatment in service to restore physically.	Matt 4:23; 8:7; 9:35; John 5:10; Acts 28:9
iatros	"healer, doctor"	"medical doctor"	One who effects healing.	Matt 9:12; Mark 5:26; Luke 4:23; Col 4:14
sozo	from saz, "safe," thus "make whole"	"heal, save, make complete".	To save from disease or oppression, keep safe and sound.	Mark 5:23; Acts 14:9

2. The word "healing" in the Classics signified "to cure, restore" in the medical sense and metaphorically. A iatros, "healer" (derived from iama) was a doctor. The historical development of "doctor" occurred in Greece (ej. The Hippocratic Oath in 400 BC, which continues valid until today). The kings were considered High Priests with the authority to heal. Until the time of Shakespeare this concept dominated: "The King touches you, God heals you" (Macbeth IV, 3).

3. In the OT (LXX), iaomai translates the Hebrew verb rapa', "to heal, or cure." For the Jews only God could heal (Ex 15:26; 2 Ki 5:7). To trust in a doctor was to deny God (2 Ki 1; 2 Chron 16:12). Since the sicknesses come from God, He is the only one that can heal (Job 5:18). This concept caused a lot of internal conflicts when a just man becomes sick (Job, Psalms 38; 51; 88), but obligated a dependence upon God as the Only one that could heal (Psalm 30:3; 103:3). In the OT the priest was not considered a healer, but one who confirms if someone had been healed (Lev 13). There was a relationship between the sin and the sickness as an expression of the wrath of God (Psalm 31:1; 38:3; 39). The healing is used as an illustration of the forgiveness of God (Isa 6:10; Psalms 30:3; 41:5; 103:3).

4. In the NT, the word is used 26 times (20 times in the Synoptic Gospels). It is interchanged with therapeuo. They were considered signs of the coming of the Messiah (Lu 9:2, 11, 42; Ac 10:38), in

the fulfillment of the OT prophecies (Isa 35:3-6; 61:1). The text of the NT is very simple: "a man was healed; he arose and went to his house carrying his bed." There is not apparently any intent to magnify the healer, as is done in the world. In a healing power flowed from Jesus (Mr 5:30; Lu 6:19). In order to heal, Jesus had to give to the one that possessed the gift (i.e., the Apostles) the authorization as an instrument of His power.

5. In the extra-biblical literature there are reports of healings, but they are always associated with exaggerations and romanticism.

6. It is important to understand the purpose of this gift in order to understand the circumstances in which it pleased the Lord to manifest it. In Acts 3:6-8 Peter healed a paralytic, instantly restoring him to normal health, and thus captured the attention of the crowd. Peter took advantage of the opportunity to preach (Ac 3:12-26). Without the healing Peter would not have had the audience. Also the healing was so obvious that everyone recognized Peter as a man with the approval of God on his life.

7. The gift of healing is related to an aspect of the gift of miracles in Acts 4:22 with the phrase, "miracle of healing."

8. The imposition of hands, through prayer or a command directed at someone to be healed, or a combination of these exercised the power.

B. Explanation

1. The uses of the gift of healing in the Early Church were two:
   a. To give authority to the message and messenger that exercises the gift of healing (Acts 3; 2 Cor 12:12; Heb 2:4).
   b. Humanitarian reasons (Acts 28:8).

2. Since the majority of the reported events today as healings do not compare to the Scriptural evidences of miraculous healings (the gifted healers in the NT could heal instantly, visibly, completely and permanently – Mr 1:42; Mt 14:36), it is necessary to explain the apparent "healings" in the following forms:
   a. Demonic power (The world was full of magicians who could heal in the time of Jesus (Ac 8:9-11). This was the thinking of the accusers of Jesus (Mt 12:24) and Simon (Acts 5).
   b. The psychosomatic power that can effect a physiological reaction, which can appear as a disorder or can be relieved with a suggestion.
      1) Today medics attribute 75% of the reported sicknesses to psychosomatic origin.
      2) If someone is convinced, with sufficient mental force, of a guaranteed remedy, suddenly the symptoms disappear.
      3) If the healer says "Have faith and more faith in order to be healed," then he is insisting in being convinced psychologically.
      4) If a healing results from such practices, it is not necessarily of God, even if it will be announced as a miracle.

3. The characteristics of healing in the Bible.
   a. The gift implies a given authority, not just a power of prayer (Acts 3:2, 5-6, 8). "I'll give you what I have." Peter gave the order for the paralytic to be healed, without prayer. He had the authority to heal delegated to him by Jesus.
   b. It is a creative power! The persons healed immediately had new physical parts, recently created. When Peter healed "...instantly the man's feet and ankles became strong" (Acts 3:7) as new muscles were created. In 2 Kings 5:14 the physical flesh of a leper having been healed instantaneously is described in detail: "his flesh came again like unto the flesh of a little child."
   c. It is occasionally a power over demons. In Luke 13:10-16 a person is deformed physically by demonic oppressive power. Upon releasing the demon from the person the deformity immediately disappears.

4. There are four observations concerning healings of sicknesses:
  a. The sickness can be an instrument of God (2 Cor 12:7-9) with a beneficial spiritual purpose. There is no obligation on God's part to heal every physical sickness. Paul continued to suffer a physical malady, which God chose not to heal, though Paul prayed for healing three times.
  b. There is no command to heal. It should be noted that none of the sign gifts are imperatives, but all of the other gifts are commanded to be manifested and practiced among believers to each other.
  c. There is very little emphasis on healing in the Epistles. Except for 1 Cor 12:9, 28, 30, no other Epistle mentions healing except James and this is not a reference to the gift of healing, rather the instructions on the ministry of praying for healing in the church.
  d. There is a description of the responsibility given to the elders (pastors) to pray for the sick (James 5:14-16). The following instructions are given for this ministry:
    1) The sick person, asking for a visit to his house initiates the petition.
    2) The elders (pastors) are told to visit the sick in his home.
    3) The oil is poured over the sick person (either ceremonially or medicinally). The act is a symbol of acceptance in Luke 7:46. If the sickness indicates a "worldliness" or a feeling of rejection from God, the oil would communicate acceptance from the church leaders. It could also be used medicinally (Luke 10:34; Isa 1:6).
    4) The confession of sins is urged to secure a clean conscience. The implication is that there is a possibility that the sickness could be the result of chastisement of God (1 Cor 11:29-31). The confession is designed to restore the person to full communion with God and the church.
    5) The prayer for healing. The words "availeth much" (KJV), or "has great power and wonderful results" (NLT) (5:16), translates the word *energoumene*, means that it "actively or really works."

C. Symptoms

1. Since the sign gifts are not able to be developed or are partially present, there are no unusual symptoms. One has the gift totally, or not at all. The gift of healing cannot be improved upon.
2. Although there are no exegetical bases for the ceasing of healings, the principal reason for their existence, that is, the authentication of the message and messenger of the new revelation of the NT, now does not exist. Everything has been confirmed beyond any historical doubt and the new revelation has been universally accepted among believers as the Word of God (1 Thes 2:13).
3. With or without the existence of the gift of healing, there is no impediment, rather encouragement, for the leadership of the church to pray for the sick that they would be healed. When the healing is for the good of the person, God will effect the healing (Rom 8:28; 1 Jn 5:14-15).

17. Tongues

A. Definitions

1. Study of the word and associated words:

Greek	Etymology	Translation	Basic Idea	Passages
glossa	"tongue"	"languages"	A tongue, the organ; a communicated language, esp. plural	James 3:5; Phil 2:11; 1 Cor 12:10, 28, 30; 13:1; 14:5; 6:18, 22, 23, 39; Acts 2:3; 1 Cor 12:10, 30; 13:8; 14:5, 6; 18; 39; 22; Rev 10:11; 17:15
			Term used to describe ecstatic utterances of pagan religions	1 Cor 14:2, 4, 9, 13; 14:19, 26, 27;
fone	"sound"	"voices, language"	An actual earthly language	1 Cor 14:10; 2 Pet 2:16; Rev 5:2
dialekto	"language"	"language, dialect"	An actual earthly language	Acts 2:6, 8-11; 21:40; 22:2

2. It is the capacity given by the Spirit to speak to people in a foreign language that was previously unknown to the speaker and was used as a sign.

3. In the OT (LXX), glossas is used to translate the Hebrew word lisan, a "tongue" or spoken "language" in 100 of the 160 appearances.

4. In the NT, glossa appears 52 times referring to the organ of speaking or to a language of communication. It is used 7 times in Revelation in the phrase "every nation, tribe, people and language" (5:9; 7:9; 10:11; 11:9; 13:7; 14:6; 17:15; 16:10). When it is a reference to a language it is always a spoken contemporary language. The consistent sense of the word in the NT is an actual language unless the context indicates the organ of a tongue.

5. The key phrase to understand the term is found in 1 Cor 12:10, where they spoke "in different kinds of tongues", hetero gene glosson (pl), that is, "different families or racial languages." The first word, "different" (hetero) means that the gift grants many different types of languages, not just one special language. In 1 Cor 14 Paul distinguished between a "tongue" (singular) and "tongues" (plural). The gift of the Spirit is plural and the imitation is the singular.

6. The word glossais (pl.) is used interchangeably with dialektos, "dialects," in Acts 2, in order to refer to actual national languages spoken by people groups on earth. This is the genuine gift. In two passages in Acts when the genuine gift of "tongues" was exercised the hearers understood the message in their hometown language (Acts 2:7-12; 10:45-46) without the need of special interpretation.

B. Explanation

1. The purpose of the gift:
   a) As with other sign gifts, tongues were used to authenticated the messenger, especially before Jewish unbelievers (1 Cor 14:21-22), who were promised a sign that they would be addressed in

"foreign languages" (Isa 28:11-12). The word in 1 Cor 14:21 is *en heteroglossois* (pl.), "by people of foreign languages." Paul specifically called the gift a "sign" (14:22) for unbelievers, especially Jews. As a sign it was useful in three instances in Acts (2; 10; 19). Never is there any insinuation of a mystical or ecstatic language.

b) The sign is not effective for evangelizing Gentile unbelievers, because they are not going to understand the significance of the promised sign (1 Cor 14:23). It is useful only to the Jews that are aware of the prophecy of Isaiah 28.

c) When the apostles had their positions accredited before the Early Church and before all the distinct Jewish national groups integrated into the church, specially the Jews in the beginning (Acts 15:8-9) the gift of tongues ceased gradually (1 Cor 13:8), just as Paul said it would.

d) When the canon of all the revelation of God in the NT was complete (1Cor 13:9-10) and when the church matured through its independence from Judaism (1 Cor 13:11) by coming to depend upon the written Word instead of Jewish apostles, the gift of tongues ceased along with prophecy and the word of knowledge (1 Cor 13:8).

2. The gift of tongues is not a sign of maturity or of spirituality. The most carnal and immature church in the NT was the only church, which had an emphasis on tongues. It was the most problematic church for Paul.

3. The gift of tongues is not a sign of the baptism of the Spirit. There is no command to be baptized by the Spirit, because it is simultaneous with, and an essential part of, our salvation (1 Cor 12:13). It is the operation of God that unites us to, and puts us in, Christ.

C. Observations:

1. No one should ever be discontented with their own spiritual gift, or in the manner in which God is working through him to help build up His churches. The majority of believers in the NT and in the history of the Church NEVER spoke in tongues.

2. Neither the church, nor individuals should emphasize a gift that is categorized as the most inferior (1 Cor 12:31). Paul ignored any reference to the gift of tongues in 12 of his 13 epistles that he wrote and never associated it with the Christian life, nor the filling of the Spirit.

3. All the spiritual gifts, even tongues, are to be for the benefit of the whole church, not for the edification or benefit of the individual (1 Cor 12:7; 10:33). Self-edification was one of the problematic abuses of the Corinthian church, which violated the principles of the gifts, thus provoking the corrections in 1 Cor 14.

4. We should follow the example of Paul who said that he would not speak in tongues in his prayers, nor singing (devotional?) (1 Cor 14:14-15), nor practice it in the church (14:19).

5. Any tongue must be accompanied by an interpretation, either by the hearers understanding their own language (Acts 2), or another person with the miraculous sign gift of interpretation of tongues, who would then relate the message to the church or listeners. Only then could there be any benefit to a tongue. It is the meaning of the message, not the experience, which has value. Without such an interpretation, tongues cannot be permitted (1 Cor 14:28). This implies that prior to permitting anyone to speak in a tongue, someone with the gift of interpretation must be recognized and on hand.

6. The Scriptures obligate the limit of tongues speakers to two or three in any given meeting (1 Cor 14:27).

7. The speakers are obligated to speak one at a time without any interruptions either from other interpreters or other speakers of tongues (1 Cor 14:27).

8. Tongues are to be spoken only by men (1 Cor 14:34).

D. Symptoms

1. The genuine gift of tongues, since it is spontaneous, cannot be developed. Like all the sign gifts, either it is genuine and miraculous, or it is an imitation and false. Any notion of "baby talk" as one begins to practice a tongue, is all symp-

toms of the false tongue.

2. The ability to speak multiple languages after exposure to and specific study of those languages should be seen more as a talent than a spiritual gift.

3. The genuineness of this gift should be demonstrated linguistically as any other language analysis. The argument that it is a "heavenly language," therefore, defies any human linguistic analysis is illogical and an attempt to escape the obvious. This absurd logic is designed to annul any criticism of contemporary tongues speaking, which only raises suspicions of its inauthenticity. No contemporary tongues speaking has ever been demonstrated to be a genuine language.

18. Interpretation of tongues

A. Definition

1. The study of the words

Greek	Etymology	Translation	Basic Idea	Passages
hermeneuo	"explain or translate"	"interpret"	Translation of a foreign idea into a familiar language.	Heb 7:2; John 1:42; 9:7
hermeneia	"explanation or translation"	"interpret"	Explain a language not known.	1 Cor 12:10; 14:26
diermeneia	"translation"	"translator"	Someone who can translate a foreign language.	1 Cor 14:27, 28, 30; Luke 24:27

2. The gift of interpretation is the supernatural ability to understand and miraculously interpret for the church a message originally delivered in a language unknown to anyone in the church, even to the interpreter. The importance of this gift is seen in Paul's description of the gift of tongues. He communicates the only value of the "tongue" is the interpretation that either a translator who knows the language spoken in the tongue, or one with the gift of interpretation who should interpret it to others (1 Cor 14:5-13).

3. Interpretation in the OT is a special gift for understanding visions and dreams. The only ones mentioned are Joseph and Daniel. There are no other references to interpreters.

4. There is no example of the use of this gift in the NT, however, Paul established its function in the Early Church (1 Cor 14:5, 13-19, 27-28). The ONLY edification possible through the gift of tongues comes when the unknown language message is interpreted and thus understood by the speaker of the original tongue, as well as all other listeners.

B. Explanation

1. The presence of someone with the gift of interpretation is imperative BEFORE it is permitted to speak in a tongue, which no one understands. For this reason this person must be previously identified. The implication is that this gift can interpret any language.

2. It seems that this gift of interpretation is associated with that of prophecy, that is, through this gift the revelation of God and the mysteries were communicated to the hearers (1 Cor 13:2; 14:2, 6, 30). The difference was that the gift of interpretation depended upon the gift of tongues for the receipt of the revelation.

C. Symptoms

1. This sign gift cannot be developed since it is a miraculous understanding of another sign gift of tongues, which was completely unknown to the interpreter.

2. As with other miraculous gifts, it probably disappeared along with the gift of tongues in the first century as history affirms.

3. A convincing proof of the genuineness of this gift could easily be demonstrated if two persons with the gift of interpretation independently heard a language unknown to them, then gave identical translations of what was said. This has never been demonstrated.

Analysis of the use tongues as a mystical prayer language

The most common use of tongues in the contemporary charismatic churches is the private or "devotional" practice of communicating to God in a special language. The user is totally ignorant of what is communicated. It is said that through the gift of tongues one can better communicate with God in prayer by using a personal and intimate language that only God understands. The speaker supposedly "edifies" himself by praying in a "tongue," which he does not understand.

The practice of a devotional or secret tongue is creeping into many non-Pentecostal churches and ministries. There is little or no teaching on the subject of the gifts or tongues in most churches, while members are constantly exposed to charismatic teaching through the media, friends and visiting other churches. These members can be persuaded to begin practicing concepts or habits that might not be in accord with the Scriptures.

The purpose of this review is to clarify the NT teachings on the practice and meaning of tongues for the believers and churches.

A. The idea of "devotional tongues" is based on insinuation, not on clear teachings.

In the entire NT there is no clear declaration that the gift of tongues would have any private use for the user. The only examples of tongues are public (Acts 2, 10, 19). Paul corrected the church at Corinth for its misuse of the gift of tongues and the statements of their abuses are taken as acceptable practices. These verses will be explained later.

B. Devotional tongues are contrary to the purpose of the spiritual gifts.

All the spiritual gifts are given to benefit others. They are not for the recipient of the gifts. The NIV puts it this way; "to each one the manifestation of the Spirit is given for the common good" (1 Cor 12:7, NIV). Another translation states the purpose of the gifts, "as a means of helping the entire church."

The use of the gifts is consistent. Can you imagine the gift of giving to benefit one's self? Or show mercy to one's self? Or to help or serve one's self? Always in every case, the benefactor of the exercise of a gift is another person or the church. The teaching that the private use of a devotional tongue for personal edification is completely egoistic: it is used to feel better, to feel closer to God, to have a supposed better communication with God, or to have a new experience with God.

Does this mean, therefore, that only a few can have intimate communication with God? Something seems wrong with this view. If these purposes were Biblical, then the gift of tongues or devotional tongues should be given to every believer, but the Bible teaches that none of the gifts are for everyone. "Does everyone have the gift of healing? Does God give all of us the ability to speak in unknown languages? Can everyone interpret unknown languages? No!" (1 Cor 12:30, NLT). God never intended that all believers should speak in tongues for any reason, nor should any other single gift be distributed to all believers.

The principle given in the context of the spiritual gifts in 1 Cor 13:1-4 obligates that the gifts be exercised in love (*agape*). This is not an emotional experience, but rather a commitment to benefit and minister to others (13:4-7). In this text Paul specifically declared that love "is not self-seeking" (NIV), that is the gifts of the Spirit when motivated by love will not be for personal benefit, but rather for others. All of the gifts empower ministries for others, never for one's self.

C. Devotional tongues are contrary to the purpose of genuine gift of tongues

In Mark 16:15-17 Jesus said that certain signs would follow the ministries of His disciples. One of those signs was "tongues." The primary purpose is that "speaking in tongues is a sign, not for believers, but for unbelievers" (1 Cor 14:22, NIV). In Acts 2:4-11 appears a clear example of the use of tongues as a sign to unbelieving Jews.

The multilingual Jews from all over the Mediterranean world who were present in Jerusalem at the Feast of Pentecost heard the message preached in many of their own particular dialect. Such a linguistic demonstration would be impossible for anyone living in Galilee all his life.

Seven or more years later the sign in Acts 10:46 was the identical sign which equated for the first time that the Gentile converts could equally received the Holy Spirit, just as the disciples of Acts 2. It was evident that the Gentile converts should be considered on an equal basis with the Jewish disciples. There was no difference in the sign, so there should be no difference in their relationship to God. Once the same miraculous sign proved this equality, then there was no need for the sign to be repeated again and again. Once the sign fulfilled its purpose there was no need for a repetition.

In Acts 19:6, a group of followers of John the Baptist, a separate repentant group of Jewish believers awaiting the kingdom and Messiah, heard the gospel and accepted the gospel message. As a sign that they were receiving the same Holy Spirit and thus would be part of the same Church as the Jewish and Gentile converts to Christ, they too were momentarily able to speak in a language that they did not understand. Once it was clear that even the disciples of John had to be saved through believing in Christ, it was never again necessary to be proven by a special sign. Now everyone and every people group knew that salvation was only through Christ and it was for everybody, Jews (Acts 2), all Gentiles (Acts 10) and those Hellenistic Jews expecting the Messianic kingdom as the disciples of John (Acts 19).

The private devotional use of tongues is never described in the NT, nor is it possible to be a sign to unbelievers, which is the stated purpose of the gift. Also the existence of the gift of interpretation of tongues, a necessary compliment to the gift of tongues, so there would be some benefit from a spoken tongue language, implies that God would not have needed this gift of interpretation if the primary use of the gift of tongues was to be used as a "devotional tongue."

D. Tongues was never to be a sign to the speaker

The "devotional tongues" are not to minister to others, by definition, but should be a sign to someone (14:22), but to whom? It would have to be a sign to the speaker himself. If it is a sign, then what is it a sign of? The only thing that it could signal would be the certainty that the speaker has the Holy Spirit indwelling him. However, any of the spiritual gifts would indicate that the Spirit is indwelling.

The genuine confidence that the Holy Spirit is indwelling should be understood and derived from the promise of the Spirit by faith in the promises of the Scriptures, not from an experience however impressive. Thus as a sign to the speaker himself, it does not make sense nor does it have a Biblical purpose.

E. Tongues are not for self-edification

The idea of "self-edification" comes from misunderstanding of 1 Cor 14:3-4, "One who speaks in a tongue edifies himself." This is not a praise for self-edification, rather it is given as a reason why tongues are less important than the edification purpose of prophesy. Paul was not affirm the legitimacy of the Corinthian believer's experience as being from the Holy Spirit. One might even say that irony is to be found in Paul's statement.

"It should be carefully noted that if Paul is not using irony here, then he is crediting very carnal believers with an intimacy with the Holy Spirit and with God, with deep spiritual experiences. All of his other writings, and all the rest of Scripture, teach most emphatically that a carnal believer can never enter into this kind of relationship.... He most definitely is using irony as a weapon to lay bare the emptiness of the claims of carnal believers."

Paul's whole argument presumes an abuse or error in usage of the gift of tongues in the Corinthian church. Whenever Paul contrasts tongues with prophecy, he is consistently pointing out the weaknesses and wrong application of tongues among the Corinthians.

The word "edify" can be used both negatively and positively. An illustration of the negative use is in 1 Cor 8:10 , "For if anyone with a weak conscience sees you who have this knowledge eating in an idol's temple, won't he be emboldened to eat what has been sacrificed to idols?" The conscience of the "weak" brother can be "emboldened" or "stimulated" to eat something offered to idols. This is the same word, *oikodomeo*. This is negative edification. It could be argued that their use of tongues was motivating or emboldening them, not for spiritual, but carnal values. The context would support this concept in stead of the idea that their use of tongues was making them more spiritual.

"The very characteristic of the Corinthians' heathen past, [Paul] argues, was the sense of being overpowered and carried away by spiritual forces…. "There is no doubt at all," Schrenk comments, "that Paul intends to say here that the truly spiritual person is not marked by a being swept away… that was precisely the characteristic of previous fanatical religions." It is important to notice that Paul places this evaluation of the spiritual "sweeping away" at the very outset of his treatment of "spiritual things" in Corinth (12:2). "As the super scripture to his essay in chapters twelve to fourteen Paul has written: 'Seizure is not necessarily Christian or spiritual.'"

1. There are several reasons why the "edification" in 1 Cor 14:4 should be understood negatively. There were divisions in the church as a result of pride and self-glorification (1:26-29; 3:3-7, 18, 21). They were proud of their giftedness, especially the gift of tongues.

2. In the context of chapter 14 Paul made it clear that it is impossible to positively edify yourself by the use of a tongue, because no one could understand the tongue. In 14:5 Paul declared that no one could be edified (positively) without understanding what was said. In 14:6 Paul concluded that neither could the speaker be edified until his tongue was interpreted. In 14:9 speaking in a tongue was "speaking into the air", that is, without any benefit to anybody. When the hearer does not understand the tongue, even in a prayer (14:16), no edification takes place! (14:17). The conclusion is clear that there is no biblical edification through the use of a tongue unless and until it is interpreted.

3. The speaker himself "is unfruitful" (14:14) until it is interpreted. Thus to pray without understanding what is being said (as in a tongue) is "unfruitful" or a negative action of self-deception, without any personal benefit. The paradox of the Corinthian church is that they were priding themselves and deceiving themselves in what was really useless before the Lord.

4. A lack of understanding (14:6) is equal to the lack of edification (14:17). Two times in the context (14:5, 17) Paul clarified that edification is impossible without understanding of the Word of God. If the mind is not functioning in order to understand the new knowledge revealed, a new truth, exhortation, consolation or practical application, Biblical edification has not occurred. There is nothing to respond to obey or for which to praise God, since nothing is understood.

5. God designed the gifts to generate an interdependence, so that we could be edified through the ministry of others, not that we could edify ourselves (Eph 4:16). The concept of independent edification does not appear in the Scriptures, in fact, the notion is contrary to every principle of edification in the NT. The church body is edified by the exercise of the teaching and exhorting gifts to keep growing in its walk with God corporately and individually.

6. The only supposed value of speaking in a tongue is (a) to recognize a God given gift and (2) some emotional satisfaction. These "experiences" are considered "edification." However, the possessor of the gift of prophecy could recognize that God had given him a gift and he could even feel an emotion because God was speaking through him, but it was never for self-edification. The satisfaction that comes from exercising any gift is the benefit produced in the lives of others. The idea that God would give a gift to some for their personal experience or a privileged sense of having received something special from God is useless for edification.

7. The concept of edification in the NT is dependent upon increasing understanding of the Word along with the application to one's personal life through exhortation, knowledge, comfort, cor-

rection, clarification or instruction. The books of the NT were written with this style: first to establish the truth (Rom 1-11; Eph 1-3), and then the application or exhortation based on the truth already understood (Rom 12-16; Eph 4-6). Never are we exhorted to feel something or have an experience in order to be edified. The concept that an emotion or sensation of being used by God is edification is not of a Biblical origin or concept.

8. In the Bible the believers never are exhorted or motivated to edify themselves through the spiritual gifts. There are many Scriptural passages that refer to edification and exhortation, but none make any reference to or benefit of tongues (Eph 4:11 gives a list of gifts or gifted men whose purpose is to edify).

9. This self-edification, for the few that receive the miraculous capacity to grow spiritually, is not available for all those who have not received this gift. This idea inevitably creates an "elite" of the "spiritual." The idea of a special power for the few to be able to grow spiritually is totally contrary to the NT. If anyone says that the gift is for everyone who wants it, then his teaching is likewise contrary to the NT: no spiritual gift is for everyone.

10. Paul probably is saying that the one who speaks in a tongue to "edify himself" with no intention of edifying others, is simply "exalting" himself. No one has been able to explain how an unintelligible language or tongue could possibly edify the person who is speaking it. It does not fulfill any of the Biblical norms of edification.

F. Tongues are not for prayer or praise

The two phrases that need clarification: first, "For one who speaks in a tongue does not speak to men, but to God" (1 Cor 14:2) and second, "if there is no interpreter, let him keep silent in the church; and let him speak to himself and to God" (14:28). These verses are used to imply that tongues speakers had a special intimate communication with God. It is essential, as always, to understand a verse in the light of its context and not independent of its context.

1. In 14:1-3 Paul is exhorting the Corinthian church to prefer prophecy over tongues in order to speak to men, instead of tongues, which could only be spoken to God, since neither the speaker, nor the hearer could understand. For this reason it is useless as a gift for edification. In the assembly, speaking to the congregation is preferable to speaking to God. The prayers and praise to God are important in the church, but only when they are understood (1 Cor 14:15-16; Eph 6:18; Phil 4:4-6; Col 4:2; 1 Thes 5:17; 1 Tim 2:1, 8).

   a) The introductory "for" in 14:2, indicates a reason for the exhortation in v. 1: to make sure that "love" motive is supreme (where others are benefited) and the priority is given to prophecy or the revelation of the Word of God. However you interpret v.2 it must be in the light of v. 1. The reason the gift of tongues (without interpretation) is of little value is because it doesn't speak to men, since no one can understand unless he knows the language. This is the same idea as to "speak in the air" (v.9). The meaning is that God is the only one that could possibly understand him... if it were a real language, or really saying something.

   b) The phrase "but to God" (v. 2) is not an absolute statement, in the sense that it describes how to speak to God or how the gift should function. The following phrase is linked by the same introductory word, gar, or "for", "Indeed no one understands him." Paul is saying that the only one who could possibly understand a foreign tongue unknown to anyone present would be God. This is not a reference to a special prayer at all or an unintelligible tongue. If someone could understand the tongue speaker, then he would be speaking to men and not to God. When the tongue was used as in the day of Pentecost (Acts 2:6-8) those present understood what was spoken, thus the speakers spoke both to man and God, since both understood. Tongues are for a sign to men (1 Cor 14:22), thus the purpose of the sign is to be understood. Since genuine tongues (real languages) are to be understood by men, 14:2 is not an absolute, that is, it is not the absolute purpose of the gift of tongues.

    c) Paul was not exalting tongues as a medium of communication with God, rather was demonstrating its limitations, especially in comparison with the gift of prophecy. Paul was not saying that tongues are for prayer and praise, but that prophecy is preferred because it is easily understood in one's own language. Tongues could be beneficial only if used correctly, that is someone understood what was spoken (either miraculously through the gift of interpretation or a foreigner understood in his language as at Pentecost). Paul sought to limit the use of tongues in the congregation. It seems apparent that the idea of speaking "only to God" was a negative concept, according to Paul. In fact, Paul made it clear that if an interpreter was not present then tongues should not even be spoken (14:28).

    d) The final phrase of "utters mysteries with his spirit" is probably a reference to the pagan practices in the mystery religions. "Among the ancient Greeks 'the mysteries' were religious rites and ceremonies practiced by secret societies into which any one who so desired might be received. Those who were initiated into these 'mysteries' became possessors of certain knowledge, which was not imparted to the uninitiated, and were called 'the perfected,'" Perhaps they were trying to imitate the pagan practices to show that they were even more spiritual than their pagan neighbors.

2. The prohibition to speak in tongues without an interpreter does not exalt tongues as a medium of communication with God: "if there is no interpreter, let him keep silent in the church; and let him speak to himself and to God" (1 Cor 14:28). However, no one can speak to himself if he doesn't understand what he is saying, so this is really not a form of communication at all. In the context of this verse Paul is obligating them to speak in a manner where it will not cause a disturbance, where only God could listen. Once again, these verses are corrective in nature, not instructive, that is, Paul is not saying that while the service is going on people should be speaking to themselves (impossible without understanding) and to God in a tongue. He is saying that no matter what you sense as a revelation or a tongue, you should not interfere with the on going congregational meeting. But, what sense is there to have a gift in order to speak to yourself in silence? If one takes this verse to support devotional tongues ("speak to God"), it must be understood in the same sense of "speak to himself." He is saying that if you are not going to have a ministry with others, do not bother the congregation. Again, these exhortations are all negative with regards to tongues; they in no wise can be understood to promote the universal practice of tongues.

3. As an instrument of prayer Paul made it clear that tongues are useless in 14:14-16. "For if I pray in a tongue, my spirit prays, but my mind is unfruitful. What is the outcome then? I shall pray with the spirit and I shall pray with the mind also; I shall sing with the spirit and I shall sing with the mind also. Otherwise if you bless in the spirit only, how will the one who fills the place of the ungifted say the 'Amen' at your giving of thanks, since he does not know what you are saying?" Paul determined to pray in his spirit, but WITH UNDERSTANDING, that is, in a language that he understood, not a tongue, since it is impossible to pray in a tongue "with understanding." As has been stated, without interpretation (v. 13) the prayer in a tongue is "unfruitful" (v. 14). This is categorical: to pray in a tongue, without an interpreter or understanding is useless, fruitless, and empty. This is why Paul ALWAYS prayed in his spirit and with his understanding in full function; he knew exactly what he was saying. When we pray both our spirits and our minds should be involved, thus a tongue by itself is useless.

4. "So what should I do?" (14:15) introduces a conclusion to form an absolute: the prayer that the speaker can understand is preferred over that which cannot be understood. Applying these general principles to private prayers, if using a tongue, they are likewise "unfruitful" (unless interpreted, but then

it would not be private). Thus there is no reason to pray in a language that you cannot understand.

5. Paul continues the argument concerning the weakness of tongues (14:16-17) to demonstrate the same principles apply concerning the prayer for thanksgiving or blessing. No one can understand, not even the one praying. If the prayer is not an expression of the heart of the individual, which it cannot be if even the one praying is ignorant of what he is saying, then God is not praised by a meaningless tongue. It makes no sense that God would give a gift in order that He could be praised without the persons even understanding what he is saying to God or even be able to participate in the praise. The believer might as well be a robot. It would be God merely praising Himself without the participation of the heart or mind of the individual. This is non-sense.

6. Some want to identify the prayer in a tongue with the phrase in Rom 8:26, "the Spirit Himself intercedes for us with groaning too deep for words" (NIV).

    a) The context implies that this applies to all believers (8:23, "we ourselves, having the first fruits of the Spirit, even we ourselves groan within ourselves, waiting eagerly for our adoption as sons, the redemption of our body"). The verses in the following context speak of foreknowledge, predestination, calling, justification and permanence of the love of Christ, all of which pertain to all believers. The verse describes the believer possessing the Holy Spirit within his body, which continues to have sinful cravings. This is the exact opposite of God's holiness and new life. Man's new nature longs for the day of full liberation at the resurrection or rapture from our sinfulness today. This longing or yearning for our full transformation is expressed as a "groaning" for our resurrected body.

    b) The phrase in 8:26, "groaning too deep for words", *stenagmois alaletois*, does not indicate speaking in tongues. The word *alaletois* is something "inexpressible, without words, impossible to communicate with words." It is not an audible sound. It is something unperceived and inexpressible by the believer. It is the groaning of the Spirit longing to be indwelling our glorified body someday. The verse says that it is the Spirit that emits the groaning, not the believer.

    c) In 8:21-22 the groanings are related to the desire for the fulfillment of the redemption when the body, the Temple of the Spirit, is free from the "slavery of corruption." The Spirit wants His temple (our body) to be perfected in the worst way.

7. The concept of a special kind of prayer for worship and praise to God has no precedence in the NT, but is common in the pagan world. Every believer has a perfect access to the throne through the death of Christ (John 14:13-14; Eph 2:18; 3:12). Nothing can improve this access. Furthermore, we have a perfect acceptance before the throne thanks to our High Priest (He 4:14-16) upon which no language could improve. Since the tongues are literal languages, which language is more spiritual? Chinese? English? Spanish? French? The Holy Spirit does help all believers in prayer (Rom 8:26), but not through a tongue, rather because He "intercedes for us." Nowhere in the Bible is there any motivation or exhortation to have a more intimate communication than what we have through Jesus Christ. It is all imagination and a bad understanding of certain passages that has motivated thousands to look for something that does not exist! There is no insinuation that the adoration of angels is better than that of men (Rev 4:11-5:14). So their supposed language is not beneficial. In fact, angels know nothing of the redemption in Christ so they cannot express what it means to redeemed sinners. Worship to God is always with understanding and is expressed in known tongues by those who have experienced and understand the redemption of Christ.

8. It is clear that tongues were to cease in a given moment (1 Cor 13:8). If tongues are for worshipping God supernaturally there is no reason for them to ever cease. This would make tongues just as important as love. But such is not the case. We are to be praising God forever, but "tongues will cease" (13:8). In Acts 10:46 Luke wrote, "…heard them speaking in tongues and praising God." It

is not clear if the Jews with Peter understood Cornelius and the others magnifying God in a tongue or if the verse refers to two different events: speaking in tongues and then magnifying God (the most probable). The passage indicates (a) the tongue was real and understandable by the Jews, but not understandable to Cornelius. This is evident because the Jews declared Cornelius' tongue to be an identical expression of a language "as at the beginning," or Pentecost, which was declared to be at least 16 distinct contemporary languages unknown to the speakers. (b) Whatever they said in a tongue is not important in the text, but that the witnesses understood what they said, and that it was a sign for the Jews that demonstrated God was equally working among the Gentiles as He had been working among the Jews. When Peter had to give an accounting of his evangelistic efforts before the apostles and church leaders in Jerusalem his explanation was precisely the same as above (see 11:15-18). The purpose is consistently for a sign to the Jews. Thus it is evident that there is no reason for using a tongue in prayer or devotions.

G. Tongues are for a ministry to unbelievers

All of the context in 1 Cor 14 exhorts against the use of tongues in the assembly. It is restricted in almost every verse. Such were the limitations placed on tongues that Paul wanted to minimize his instructions at the end by saying that he did not want to entirely prohibit the practice of tongues (14:39). Though they would eventually cease on their own accord (13:8), he did not want to be responsible for terminating their use prematurely, if they were beneficial to the church. Paul permitted their use under certain restrictions: must have an interpreter, can only speak one at a time, no more than two or three per meeting, no woman was permitted to speak in tongues, etc. Some have used these restrictions to come to the conclusion that tongues only have a function in a private use, but this ignores their strategic use outside of the congregation.

1) All biblical tongues have only one purpose.

Some authors want to make a distinction between the nature and purpose of the gift of tongues in Acts and 1 Corinthians. Such distinction is pure fabrication for the convenience of explaining certain contemporary experiences. They would say that in Acts tongues were for a sign, but in Corinth tongues were given for the public and private edification. Others would emphasize that in Acts tongues were the confirmation of the "baptism of the Spirit."

All the tongues in the NT have the same nature. It cannot be more clearly stated than in 1 Cor 14:22, "tongues are for a sign, not to those who believe, but to unbelievers." This is a categorical and absolute statement of purpose. Also in Mark 16:17, 20 it is clear that tongues are for a sign. Every time in the NT historical narratives they were used for a sign (Acts 2:4-11; 10:44-46 with 11:15-18 and 19:6). They were not sought, nor desired by the recipient, because before the event none even knew what they were.

In 1 Corinthians Paul made it clear that his use of tongues was not for the congregation, nor in his devotional life, but rather outside of the congregation. The only benefit of tongues would be a demonstration of the power and presence of God to those who could appreciate what they meant.

2) Tongues are a sign to the unbelievers

The gift of tongues is the miraculous ability to speak in another language as a demonstration of the power of God. Multilingual foreigners listening to their unique dialect could only appreciate it. There was a double miracle of a tongue and a miraculous interpretation by someone who had not been exposed previously to the language. These are the only explanations of the antecedents in the Bible (Acts 2, 10 and 19).

A purpose for a tongue such as has been defined as ecstatic utterances or a "celestial or angelic" tongue cannot be demonstrated in Scriptures. It has also been shown that "devotional tongues" has no antecedent in the Scriptures. Since the gift of tongues is a dialect of an actual language, the purpose is to communicate with people of the same language.

By elimination the gift of tongues has its chief purpose outside the congregation while prophecy has its chief function inside the congregation. In 1 Cor 14:18-19 using an exaggerated statement, hyperbole, Paul declared that as far as he was concerned tongues are not for any use in the congregation: "in the church I desire to speak five words with my mind, that I may instruct others also, rather than ten thousand words in a tongue."

The connection between verses 21-22 is interesting. "Do not be children in your thinking; yet in evil be babes, but in your thinking be mature." In this context children are going to want the gift of tongues for themselves, but all the gifts are for benefit of others. The use of tongues among believers is an indication of immaturity. If tongues are for "a sign, not to those who believe, but to unbelievers" (v. 22), then it is impossible to consider its purpose as devotional tongues or a mystical praise or communication with God. When they were used as a sign, such as on the day of Pentecost, they were effective. When they were used in the congregations, the unbeliever did not accept them as a sign (14:23), rather they thought that the believers were "crazy." In the church they are inefficient for evangelism.

3) Tongues are a sign especially to the Jewish unbelievers

In Isaiah 28:11 we have the prophecy of a sign "to this people," that is, to Israel. As a result, every time that tongues appeared in Acts it is in the presence of Jews, since the gospel was restricted to the Jews almost exclusively for the first decade years (Acts 11:19). Even when a Gentile spoke in tongues (Acts 10), it was a sign or testimony to the Jews.

However, Paul is not saying that tongues is the fulfillment of Isa 28:11, but rather that God has wanted to give the Jews a confirmation sign of what He was doing. The exact fulfillment of the prophecy in Isaiah occurred in 605 BC when Babylon invaded Israel and spoke to them in a foreign language as a sign (Jer 5:15). Since the church in Corinth was primarily Gentiles he wanted to clarify the use of tongues for the ministry.

Also Jesus declared that no sign would be given to this generation, except that of the resurrection (Mt 12:39; 16:4; Mar 8:12). The implication in 1 Cor 1:22-23 is that the Jews are anticipating a sign of confirmation, even though they were not going to receive it, so tongues were for all unbelievers in the time of the confirmation of the gospel.

4) Tongues are not a sign of the baptism of the Spirit after conversion

The teaching of the necessity of a baptism of the Spirit AFTER salvation, a second work of grace, has no Biblical foundation. However, this single doctrine is the basis of the grand schism in the Church of Christ today. From this misconception many other errors have spun off.

The baptism of the Spirit is the operation of the Spirit by which the believer is placed into the body of Christ, thereby becoming a co-participant of all that Christ is. Without the baptism of the Spirit it is impossible to be "in Christ," that is, it is impossible to be saved! Before Pentecost the disciples of Christ were believers, but did not possess the indwelling Spirit, because they had not had received the baptism of the Spirit. Today no one can repeat those conditions of having believed, but not have the Spirit, since the Spirit has been given to the world and is received as a gift in the moment of receiving Christ as Savior (Acts 2:38).

The Pentecostals want to teach that speaking in tongues is a sign for the believer to confirm he has received the baptism of the Spirit. However, we have already seen that the purpose of tongues is to be a sign to the unbelievers, not to the believers (1 Cor 14:22). There is no declaration in the Bible that tongues would be the evidence of something that would occur after salvation. In Mark 16:17-20 the tongues would be a sign for an evangelistic ministry with unbelievers, especially for the disciples of Christ. In Acts 2:4-11 appears a demonstration of the effectiveness of tongues as a sign to unbelievers, esp. Jews. The purpose was especially to convince Israel of the truth of Christ (2:36). More than seven years later, in the home of Cornelius, we see the second appearance of tongues in the history of the Church. It was not an on-going experience of believers. The reference to "as at the beginning" (14:15), with no reference to any other appearance of tongues even at Samaria (8:5-25) insinuates that nothing like the Pentecost manifestation had occurred in the seven-year interval. The event did not occur after the salvation of Cornelius, but rather at the moment of his salvation. He was not a believer before (Acts 11:14-18) and the experience resulted in the confirmation to the Jewish witnesses that they had a genuine salvation experience (compare 11:14 with 18).

In Acts 19:1-6 we find the last time that tongues appears in Acts, the record of the first 28 years of the Church. The event occurred in Ephesus almost 13 years after the conversion of Cornelius. It was another salvation experience for the Jewish disciples of John, because they had not heard anything about Jesus, nor of the coming of the Spirit. They were another group of Old Testament believers, needing a salvation experience of the new covenant.

The only reference to tongues outside of the three occurrences in Acts is in 1 Corinthians 12-14. There is no insinuation of a baptism posterior to conversion. The only reference to the baptism of the Spirit indicates that it is part of the salvation experience. Paul says, "we were all made to drink of one Spirit" (1 Cor 12:13). Paul is teaching that this is a universal experience of all believers and, in fact, is the basis of the unity of the Body. There is no suggestion that tongues were ever related to this baptism in 1 Cor 12-14.

In none of the passages that refer to tongues is there even the most remote suggestion that they are evidence of the baptism of the Spirit. The theme in each case is the formation of the Body of Christ in the moment of the salvation of individuals.

All the purposes of the gift of tongues are lost if they are a supposed sign of the baptism of the Spirit. Tongues are a literal language. Why would there be a language to demonstrate such a second blessing? The gifts are for a ministry to others, exercised in love. If tongues are evidence of an individual's baptism in the Spirit, they do not function as a gift of the Spirit where nobody else benefits. Why would there be a clear declaration of purpose as a sign to unbelievers, if it were to be a sign to believers of their supposed baptism?

If there were such a sign that the believer had received the baptism of the Spirit after his salvation, the manifestation might be useful in the congregation, but all the argument in 1 Cor 14 is contrary. If this were true, tongues would be at least as important if not more so than prophecy: but the opposite is evident in 1 Cor 14. There would be no need of an interpreter, much less the need of restricting the number of participants in a meeting to two or three, by turn, who could receive the baptism of the Spirit. If tongues are evidence of the baptism of the Spirit, why did Paul say he spoke more than the rest? If he had shown the evidence once, what was the need to repeat the evidence?

To respond to these questions, it would be necessary to invent a new purpose for the gift of tongues and also to make a distinction between the tongues in Acts and in 1 Corinthians. This is precisely what the Pentecostal/charismatic interpretation has sought to do; however, it makes no sense Biblically or logically. It is a fabrication of man's imagination to desire to have a supernatural experience, beyond what the Scriptures promise.

H. Tongues and the spiritual power of the Spirit

Some have wanted to insist that tongues produce a spiritual revival in the church. What do the Scriptures teach? Just the opposite! The single church that emphasized tongues in the NT was likewise the most carnal (1 Cor 3:1-3). Tongues never guaranteed spiritual power or vitality. They were divided, accepted immorality, suing each other in pagan courts, discriminating among themselves, being drunk at the Lord's supper, and selfishly hording their funds. If tongues were so important for the spirituality of the church why did Paul teach that it was better not to use tongues? When Paul mentioned the gifts that edify the church, why did he not make a reference to tongues (Eph 4:11)?

The principle that none of the gifts of the Spirit would be distributed throughout the Body of Christ, means that no one gift would be given to every believer (1 Cor 12:17-20). Thus it becomes impossible for every believer to ever receive the gift of tongues. This would then make it impossible for every believer to ever receive the spiritual power that is supposedly promised. Inevitably this would create a spiritual elite, the haves and have-nots. Of course, the way around this obstacle is to ignore the teachings of Paul.

The purpose of tongues has nothing to do with the spirituality of the church. In fact, none of the spiritual gifts are signs of, or guarantee of, the spiritual vitality of the church. The spiritual gifts do not guarantee infallibility or inerrancy. The gifts are Spirit empower internal motivation and give unique capability to serve the needs of others in specific areas, not necessarily spiritual vitality.

If tongues were so important for edification, why is there so little emphasis in the NT? They were never designed to signal spiritual growth. They are given to win the lost, especially the unbelieving Jews. The gifts of prophecy for producing the revealed Word of God and teaching for clarifying and applying the Word to our lives are the primary gifts for edification of believers. This is the emphasis of 1 Cor 14. By twisting the sense of the passage to mean something foreign to its original sense has caused the division in the Body of Christ.

I. The priority of the gift of tongues

The importance and priority of tongues given in many charismatic churches is similar to that of Corinth, which obligated Paul to make such strict corrections to their doctrine. In Corinth tongues was the priority, and Paul sought to minimize its practice and priority. For example, Paul said that he spoke in tongues more than any of them (1 Cor 14:18), but never wrote concerning these experiences! It does not seem very important to Paul. He made it clear by an exaggerated declaration that he would never speak in tongues in the church (14:19).

All of the thrust of 1 Cor 12-14 is to devalue the importance of tongues placing a number of restrictions on its use. There is no evidence that any other church manifested tongues except Corinth. Nowhere in the NT is there any exhortation to anybody to ever speak in tongues. Why, then, do churches today encourage and exhort believers to speak in tongues?

In 1 Cor 12:28 Paul spoke directly about the priority of the gifts, giving five categories which clearly identify the priorities by "first," "second," "third," "then" and "then." The order runs from "apostle" to "tongues." All of the gifts are not mentioned, but sufficient in order to demonstrate priority categories of the gifts. Tongues, healing and miracles are given less priority than the gift of teaching! The churches should reflect this same priority list.

The gifts that are given priority in the church are those gifts that will edify. The context of 1 Cor 14 proves that tongues have little or no value for edification. The purpose of 1 Cor 12 was to refute the idea that tongues should be emphasized and that everyone should manifest the gift of tongues. jEven when the genuine gift of tongues existed, it should not be emphasized.

J. The emphasis on seeking the gift of tongues

Since the beginning of the Pentecostal movement many have sought the gift of tongues. Many today want to speak in tongues in order to have the security of having received the "baptism of the Spirit." Several principles should be understood about seeking any of the gifts.

First of all, the gifts are sovereignly given, that is, God alone decides who receives which gifts. The desire of the believer has nothing to do with the allocation of the gifts (1 Cor 12:11, 18).

Secondly, it is evident in the context (12:12-20) one member (gift) cannot be changed for another member, or if it were possible, the sense of the passage would be lost. The Body is made up of its members, which are determined by God. To the contrary, the members would determine the Body, resulting in the monsters described in 1 Cor 12. Paul emphasized that all the gifts are important and immutable or unchangeable.

The passages that refer to seeking the gifts should be analyzed. First, no one in the Bible who spoke in tongues was seeking it. The only person who sought a gift of the Spirit is in Acts 8:18-24 when Simon, the magician, sought the power of the Spirit. He even wanted to pay for it. The principle of the passage is that it is sin to think that one can obtain a gift of God through human means or desires. It is an offense to His sovereignty.

The verses utilized for seeking the gifts are 1 Cor 12:31; 14:1, 12, 39. The word, "desire," *zeloo*, can be translated as "desire or envy", principally to say, "be jealous for". It is the root of the English word "zeal". Twelve times in the NT it is used to mean "zealous." More significant is the nuance of an attitude instead of an action.

It should be noted that the context is directed toward the entire congregation, not individuals. Paul had just demonstrated the categories and priorities of the gifts (12:28). The gifts that should be given priority and emphasis are apostles, prophets and teachers, instead of the gifts in the fifth and last category (healing, helps, administration and speaking in tongues). The attitude of the congregation is to be zealous for protecting this priority.

However, there are concepts that contradict the idea of "desire" in the sense of "seek:"

1.   The emphasis in the chapter is to be satisfied with the gift that God has given at conversion to each believer placed in the Body by the Spirit baptism. In 12:15 a member sought to change his identity. To seek a change or addition of giftedness is contrary to what Paul is teaching.
2.   Two verses clearly declare that the gifts are distributed where God wants. To seek a gift is in violation of 12:11 and 18 that teach that the believer should accept the gifts that God gives them.
3.   There are words in Greek to say "seek" (*zeteo, orgo*) and "desire" (*thelo, epithumeo and boulomai*), but they are never used in the Bible with reference to seeking a spiritual gift! Paul used these words many times (*zeteo*, 19 times; *orgo* was used for seeking the pastoral ministry in 1 Tim 3:1). The other words were used frequently also (*thelo*, 60 times; *epithumeo*, 8 times; *boulomai*, 5 times), but none of these words are used with reference to seeking the gifts.
4.   The principle of 12:31 is that the church (implied by the use of the plural form of verbs to indicate a group) should be zealous for or have enthusiasm for or emphasize certain gifts, particularly the gifts that edify.

1 Cor 14:1 and 14:39 use the same word, *zeloo*, and should be understood in the same manner. The priority of love should be manifested in all the gifts, that is, by serving others, especially through your particular gift. The context (14:1-25) has nothing to do with individuals looking for a gift; rather the church should have preference and respect for the gifts that edify.

In 14:39 the same word is used along with "to prophesize," but Paul is not saying that every individual should seek his own gift of prophecy. The individual is not in view. This is the attitude that the church as a whole should have toward the gifts that edify. Those with these edifying gifts should be highly valued and protected for their ministry to the body.

In 14:12 Paul intentionally made a difference between "emphasize or be jealous for" (*zelotai* from *zeloo*) and the word "to seek" (*zeteo*). Literally this should be translated, "since you are zealous of spiritual gifts, seek to abound for the edification of the church" (NASV). If Paul wanted to encourage the seeking of spiritual gifts such as tongues, he could have used the word that would obligate it, but he did not.

When Paul wanted individuals to desire or seek something he used the imperative singular as in 1 Tim 3:1. Here the individual should extend his efforts to be acceptable as a pastor, aspire to the ministry (*oregetai*). There are areas of ministry that should be sought, but not the spiritual gifts. When Paul wanted the believer to seek something, he exhorted the believer to desire and seek it with energy. This concept is never applied to the spiritual gifts, nor is there any other indication that someone was able to seek a spiritual gift and, as a consequence, received it. Actually, the entire context of the gifts is contrary to the concept of seeking a spiritual gift of any kind.

K. The Biblical restrictions concerning the use of the gift of tongues

If the gift of tongues is for speaking in a foreign tongue for the benefit of unbelievers (especially Jews) then it should be used before an audience of unbelieving Jews. To speak in private or in the assembly is not the best manner to use it. The genuine gift of tongues was discouraged, but permitted under certain conditions and restrictions:

1. It must edify the church (14:26) possible through interpretation.

2. No one is permitted to speak in a tongue unless an interpreter is known to be present (14:28) and immediately gives an interpretation of the tongue to the church.
3. Only two or three speakers are the maximum permitted to speak in any given meeting (14:27)
4. Those that speak in tongues have to speak in turn, never simultaneously (14:27), so everyone could get the meaning of the interpretation.
5. The women are not permitted to speak, especially in tongues (14:34-35).
6. The meeting must maintain order and never get out of control (14:33, 40).

These restrictions are applicable only to the genuine gift of languages, that speak in a literal dialect.

Conclusion

There is no proof or example that the gift of tongues brings ecstasy or speaking ecstatically with unintelligible sounds. There was no preparation for speaking in tongues, no excitation was necessary, no trance, emotion or special circumstances. The speaker is in full control of himself always and can stop anytime it is necessary (14:28, 32). The one speaking in a tongue is not more under the control of the Spirit than one exercising any other gift such as prophecy, helps or teaching. There was no the other common phenomena such as convulsions, "slaying in the Spirit" or falling to the ground, remaining motionless on the ground for long periods, foaming in the mouth, cries, jerking, prolonged laughter, waiving back and forth in a trance like state, strange tone of voice or drifting into unconsciousness were ever present in the Biblical text. However, such experiences were common among pagan sects in the first century even as today in animistic religions.

The declared purpose of the gift of tongues is a sign to unbelievers (14:22). Such purpose does not include the emphasis on devotional or private or angelic tongues. Only the capacity to speak miraculously in a real language previously unknown to the speaker is in harmony with the NT. Tongues are a foreign language used in order to win a hearing of the unbeliever for a presentation of the gospel message. This apparently was the use of the gift Paul made frequently (14:18) in all of his evangelistic travels, but was of such little importance that neither Paul nor Luke ever mentioned any of these occasions in the first 22 years of Paul's ministry.

The genuine gift of tongues has a minimum priority in the Early Church, except in Corinth, which distorted the emphasis and motivated the correction given in 1 Cor 12-14. The gifts of teaching, exhortation, leading, serving, administrating, etc. should be emphasized in the churches. The special emphasis should be placed on the gifts that edify and benefit others. This is love. The perverted emphasis is the idea that a gift would benefit the individual. This is egotism.

Since we have the Spirit helping us in our prayers already and all the time (Rom 8:26), can we improve on the Spirit's ministry through a tongue? Actually, no true believer needs any more help than he already has in Christ. The idea of needing a gift of a tongue for a better communion with God denies the value of the sufficiency of our justification in Christ and obligates an extra step in order to have a more perfect communion with God. Also the provision of the gift of interpretation indicates tongues have no purpose in isolation or in private.

The contemporary emphasis on the gift of tongues does not bring as a result a spiritual church, as is evident in the Corinthian church. The true spiritual gift was to be a ministry to others, not to one's self. Lets protect and exalt the priority of mutual edification through the teaching, exhorting and serving gifts in the church.

If the Bible really has the answers to our life's needs and seeking to be more like the Lord Jesus is the maximum fulfillment in this life, then lets not get distracted by experiences, feelings and sensations. Christ is head of the Church and His leadership is evident as He distributes His gifts for serving others even as He served his disciples.

May we ever grow in a selfless attitude of giving ourselves for the benefit of others, without pride, knowing that this attitude is what pleases our Savior. This is where we should seek our satisfaction: doing what pleases our Lord Jesus, and expands His kingdom around the world.

Section III

Analyze yourself and identify which are your spiritual gifts

1. Use the following survey over your personal convictions. Remember that if you walk in the Spirit (not in the flesh), your desires come from God.

2. Ask other **Christian friends** who understand the significance of the gifts to confirm which are your spiritual gifts.

3. Ask **someone with the gift of wisdom**, discernment, teaching or exhortation to give you some additional suggestions regarding your gifts.

4. Ask some **intimate friends** to comment on their ideas of which are your gifts.

5. Principally ask the **leaders of your church** for their observations.

Spiritual Gifts Inventory

Instructions for Responding:

1. Work through each of the following 110 statements on spiritual gifts. After each, check the appropriate box that best describes to what extent the statement accurately describes you.
2. Do not answer on the basis of what you wish were true or what another says might be true, but on the basis of what, to the best of your knowledge, is true of you.

Questions to assess your giftedness	Never (0)	Rarely (1)	Sometimes (2)	Often (3)	Always (4)
1. I enjoy working with others in determining ministry goals and objectives.					
2. People with spiritual problems seem to come to me for advice or counsel.					
3. I delight in telling lost people about what Christ has done for them.					
4. It bothers me that some people are hurting and discouraged.					
5. I have a strong ability to see what needs to be done and believe that God will do it.					
6. I love to give a significant proportion of my resources to God's work.					
7. I have a strong capacity to recognize practical needs and to do something about them.					
8. I have a clear vision for the direction of a ministry.					
9. I always feel strong compassion for those in difficult situations.					
9. I always feel strong compassion for those in difficult situations.					
10. I have a strong desire to nurture God's people.					
11. I spend a significant portion of my time each week studying the Bible.					
12. I am motivated to design plans to accomplish ministry goals.					
13. I enjoy providing biblical solutions to difficult problems in life.					
14. I have a strong attraction to lost people.					
15. I am very concerned that more people are not serving the Lord.					
16. I have a strong capacity to trust God for the difficult things in life.					
17. I am eager to financially support ministries that are accomplishing significant things for God.					
18. I enjoy helping people meet their practical needs.					
19. I find that I have a strong capacity to attract followers in my ministry.					
20. I am always motivated to sympathize with those in the midst of a crisis.					
21. I am at my best when leading and shepherding a small group of believers.					
22. I have strong insight into the Bible and how it applies to people's lives.					
23. I feel significant when developing budgets to accomplish a good plan.					
24. It seems that people generally follow my advice.					

Questions to assess your giftedness	Never (0)	Rarely(1)	Sometimes (2)	Often (3)	Always (4)
25. I find that unsaved people enjoy spending time with me.					
26. I have a strong desire to encourage Christians to mature in Christ.					
27. I delight in the truth that God accomplishes things that seem impossible to most people.					
28. God has greatly blessed me with life's provisions in order to help others.					
29. I enjoy making personal sacrifices to help others.					
30. I prefer to lead people more than follow them.					
31. I delight in extending a hand to those in difficulty.					
32. I enjoy showing attention to those who are in need of care and concern.					
33. I am motivated to present God's truth to people so that they better understand the Bible.					
34. I am at my best when creating an organizational structure for a plan.					
35. I feel that I can give a biblical response to difficult situations.					
36. I derive extreme satisfaction when lost people accept Christ.					
37. I have been effective at inspiring believers to a stronger faith.					
38. I am convinced that God is going to accomplish something special through me or my ministry.					
39. I am convinced that all I have belongs to God, and I am willing to use it for his purposes.					
40. I work best when I serve others behind the scenes.					
41. If I am not careful, I have a tendency to dominate people and situations.					
42. I am a born burden-bearer.					
43. I have a deep desire to protect Christians from people and beliefs that may harm them.					
44. I am deeply committed to biblical truth and people's need to know and understand it.					
45.I delight in staffing a particular ministry structure.					
46. I have a strong sense my solutions to problems are the best application of God's Word.					
47. I feel a deep compassion for people who are without Christ.					
48. I have the ability to say the right things to people who are experiencing discouragement.					
49. I am rarely surprised when God turns seeming obstacles into opportunities for ministry.					
50. I feel good when I have opportunity to give from my abundance to people with genuine needs.					
51. I have a strong capacity to serve people.					
52. I am motivated to be proactive, no passive, in my ministry for Christ.					

Questions to assess your giftedness	Never (0)	Rarely(1)	Sometimes (2)	Often (3)	Always (4)
52. I am motivated to be proactive, no passive, in my ministry for Christ.					
53. I have the ability to feel the pain of others who are suffering.					
54. I get excited about helping new Christians grow to maturity in Christ.					
55. Whenever I teach a Bible class, the size of the group increases in number.					
56. I am good at using a ministry's resources in solving its problems.					
57. I have the ability to patiently listen to people's problems and with a few questions help them see their real issue.					
58. Training and helping others to share their faith is high on my list of priorities.					
59. People who are struggling emotionally or spiritually say I am an excellent listener.					
60. I delight in trusting God in the most difficult of circumstances.					
61. I have the capacity to give of myself as well as my possessions to help others.					
62. I am good at doing seemingly insignificant tasks to free people up for vital ministries.					
63. Most people place a lot of trust in me and my leadership.					
64. I have a desire to make a significant difference in the lives of troubled people.					
65. I enjoy being around believers and encouraging them to trust Christ for their circumstances.					
66. I have a desire to search the Bible for truths that apply to my life and the lives of others.					
67. I like monitoring plans that accomplish ministry goals.					
68. My delight is to master Proverbs and the commands of Scripture to know how to help people know how to think and act.					
69. Over the years I have prayed much for my non-Christian friends.					
70. I spend a significant amount of time exhorting believers to make Christ Lord of their lives.					
71. I am able to trust God in situations when most others have lost all hope.					
72. Friends worry that some people take advantage of my generosity with my possessions.					
73. I am motivated to accomplish tasks that most people consider insignificant.					
74. People are confident in my abilities to help them accomplish their ministry goals.					
75. Suffering people are attracted to me and find me comforting to be around.					

Questions to assess your giftedness	Never (0)	Rarely(1)	Sometimes (2)	Often (3)	Always (4)
76. I have the ability and courage to confront Christians about sin in their lives.					
77. God has given me unusual ability to explain deep biblical truths to his people.					
78. I prefer that a ministry's affairs be conducted in an orderly and efficient manner.					
79. Discerning the root cause of people's problems comes easy to me.					
80. I am deeply motivated to address the doubts and questions of lost people.					
81. I have the ability to confront disobedient Christians and see them change.					
82. People who dream big dreams for God motivate me.					
83. People regularly come to me with requests for help in meeting their financial needs.					
84. I look for opportunities to serve the practical needs of God's ministries.					
85. I am happiest in a ministry when I am able to exert a strong influence in the group.					
86. People close to me believe that I allow "down and outers" to take advantage of me.					
87. Christians often seek me out for counsel regarding important decisions in their lives.					
88. I have a strong desire to study and explain the truths of the Bible in depth.					
89. I am convinced that paying attention to details is very important.					
90. I have the sense of being able to see issues clearly when others are confused about what is the best choice of action to take.					
91. I feel a strong attraction toward evangelistic ministries.					
92. I could easily spend much of my time encouraging people in their walk with Christ.					
93. People who never take risks frustrate me.					
94. I find it difficult to understand why Christians do not give more help to those with real needs.					
95. I prefer to remain behind the scenes helping people with practical matters.					
96. I have a strong desire to take charge in most situations.					
97. I delight in visiting people in hospitals or nursing homes.					
98. I pray constantly for people who look tome for care.					
99. I have observed that people who sit under my teaching experience changed lives.					

Questions to assess your giftedness	Never (0)	Rarely (1)	Sometimes (2)	Often (3)	Always (4)
100. I have a strong desire to see people work together to accomplish their goals.					
101. My confidence in the instruction in God's Word give me assurance about giving advice that comes from the Bible.					
101. My confidence in the instruction in God's Word give me assurance about giving advice that comes from the Bible.					
102. I get extremely frustrated when I cannot share my faith.					
103. cI find great satisfaction in reassuring Christians of their need to walk with Christ.					
104. People are amazed at my ability to trust God to provide in the most difficult situations.					
105. When I give significantly to help others, I do not expect anything in return.					
106. I am convinced that no job is too menial if it truly helps people.					
107. In meetings, people look to me for the final opinion regarding a matter.					
108. I believe strongly in giving those who fail a second and even a third chance.					
109. I enjoy visiting people in their homes and when they are in the hospital.					
110. I am greatly challenged by people's questions about the Bible.					

Instructions for Scoring

1. Place the number from each of your answers on the line corresponding to the question number.
2. Add the numbers horizontally and place the total for each row in the space before each gift.

1. __ 12.__ 23.__ 34.__ 45.__ 56.___ 67.__ 78.___89.___100. __ = ___ Administration
2. ___13.__ 24.__ 35.___46.___ 57.___68. __ 79.__ 90.___ 101. ___= ___ Wisdom or Counseling
3.__ 14.__ 25.__ 36.__ 47.__ 58.__ 69.__ 80.__ 91.__ 102.__ = ___ Evangelism
4.__ 15.__ 26.__ 37.__ 48.__ 59.__ 70.__ 81.__ 92.__ 103.__ = ___ Encouragement
5.__ 16.__ 27.__ 38.__ 49.__ 60.__ 71.__ 82.__ 93.__ 104.__ = ___ Faith
6.__ 17.__ 28.__ 39.__ 50.__ 61.__ 72.__ 83.__ 94.__ 105.__ = ___ Giving
7.__ 18.__ 29.__ 40.__ 51.__ 62.__ 73.__ 84.__ 95.__ 106.__ = ___ Helps/Serving
8.__ 19.__ 30.__ 41.__ 52.__ 63.__ 74.__ 85.__ 96.__ 107.__ = ___ Leadership
9.__ 20.__ 31.__ 42.__ 53.__ 64.__ 75.__ 86.__ 97.__ 108:__ = ___ Mercy
10.__ 21.__ 32.__ 43.__ 54.__ 65.__ 76.__ 87.__ 98.__ 109.__ = ___ Pastor
11.__ 22.__ 33.__ 44.__ 55.__ 66.__ 77.__ 88.__ 99.__ 110.__ = ___ Teacher

Instructions for Determining Your Spiritual Gifts

1. Place the names of your five highest scoring gifts in the spaces below under Spiritual Gifts Inventory.

2. Place the names of any other gifts or talents that are not identified in this inventory yet are present in your life under the title Other Spiritual Gifts.

Spiritual Gifts Inventory   **Other Spiritual Gifts**

1._____   _____

2._____   _____

3. _____   _____

4. _____   _____

5. _____   _____

Instructions for Determining Your Gift-Mix and Gift-Cluster

1. To determine your gift-mix, place the names of your five highest gifts in descending order in the space below titled Gift-Mix.

2. To determine if you have a gift-cluster, decide if the first gift or another one in your mix is dominant and supported by the other gifts. If this is the case, place it kin the center space under the title Gift-Cluster and place the other gifts in the spaces surrounding it.

Gift-Mix

1. _____

2. _____

3. _____

4. _____

5. _____

Dominant _____   _____

_____

Sub-dominant _____   _____

Comments:

Opinion of Friends

Instructions: Please answer these questions as best you can to encourage and help focus your friend for a meaningful life fulfilling his spiritual giftedness.

1. What ministry have you observed your friend being involved in?

2. What is the most effective ministry area you have observed of all that he/she is doing?

3. Do you get the sense that your friend is especially gifted to be fulfilling these ministries? Can you say why you have this perspective?

4. How has your friend helped or been a blessing to you?

5. Are there areas your friend is involved in that he/she is not specially gifted to fulfill?

6. Would you say your friend has a speaking gift or a serving gift?

7. What would you recommend your friend apply himself/herself to focus on over the next few years?

… Over his/her career?

Opinion of Friends

Please answer these questions as best you can to encourage and help focus your friend for a meaningful life fulfilling his spiritual giftedness.

1. What ministry have you observed your friend being involved in?

2. What is the most effective ministry area you have observed of all that he/she is doing?

3. Do you get the sense that your friend is especially gifted to be fulfilling these ministries? Can you say why you have this perspective?

4. How has your friend helped or been a blessing to you?

5. Are there areas your friend is involved in that he/she is not specially gifted to fulfill?

6. Would you say your friend has a speaking gift or a serving gift?

7. What would you recommend your friend apply himself/herself to focus on over the next few years?

… Over his/her career?

Opinion of Church leaders

Please answer these questions as best you can to encourage and help focus your friend for a meaningful life fulfilling his spiritual giftedness.

1. What ministry have you observed your friend being involved in?

2. What is the most effective ministry area you have observed of all that he/she is doing?

3. Do you get the sense that your friend is especially gifted to be fulfilling these ministries? Can you say why you have this perspective?

4. How has your friend helped or been a blessing to you?

5. Are there areas your friend is involved in that he/she is not specially gifted to fulfill?

6. What would you recommend your friend apply himself/herself to focus on over the next few years?

… Over his/her career?

Section IV.

Guidance from experience

Instruction: Let your experience be a determining factor in the manifestation of your gifts.

1. Your church will be more and more conscience of your gifts as you work in its programs.
2. You will be conscious of the fruit that results from the exercise of your gift in the lives of others.
3. You will feel a conscious satisfaction in what you are doing.
4. You will recognize that those with gifts, especially the gift of leadership, are going to attract others with similar gifts.
5. Complete the survey of your personal experiences.

Personal Experience Survey

1. What ministries are you currently involved in?

2. What ministries have given you the most satisfaction or fulfillment?

3. Which ministries have you received the most positive feedback from others?

4. What ministry for other are you the most motivated to repeat or get involved in?

5. If you could do anything to help others, what would you want to do?

6. If you knew you would be successful and would not lack any resources, what would you like to see accomplished in your life that would most honor and glorify the Lord?

Section V.

A plan of action

The gifts that have been chosen must be put into practice. Begin with the suggested plan of development of your gifts. Choose a ministry area in the sphere of your gifts and commit yourself to use them from now on.

1.   Follow the procedures that are recommended according to the gifts chosen.
2.   Write in your own words a plan for how you will seek to develop your gifts.
3.   Write the area or type of service that you will seek to fulfill in the future.
4.   Write the desire of your heart about what you want to complete for the Lord with your gifts or ministries.

The design of God in creating the ever-growing body of Christ as new believers join the church is to allow them to find a meaningful and productive function in their service for the Savior. Leaders are trainers and facilitators (Eph 4:12) of the multiple ministries of each of the believers in their congregation.

Administration

Symptoms and definitions:

The desire and ability to see clearly how to have the right people doing the right things to accomplish their God-given goals and objectives, by organizing and supervising others. They love strategic planning, facilitating different ministries to make them more effective, and to bring order and confidence in any group. Without these gifted persons chaos and frustration is common. They are the managers that turn the vision of leaders into reality, and love doing it.

A recommended procedure for developing this give would include:

- Identify persons with the gift of administration that you admire.
- Dialogue with them about how they seem to know how to organize themselves and others
- Inquire about how they learned the skill and disciplines of administration
- Ask your Bible class, church organization or activity if you could help them get organized or supervised to make sure things happen well and timely.
- Learn the art of accountability with every relationship.

Areas or type of service could include the following areas:

Congregation Council, Finance Staff, Sunday School Superintendent, Vacation Bible School Coordinator, Business Manager, organizing class or church activities or functions, managing Short-Term mission trips,

Which of these appeal to your interests: _____

Write out the desires of your heart of what you want to do for the Lord with this gift:

_____

_____

What are you going to begin doing this week to practice this gift?

_____

_____

Mercy

Symptoms and definitions:

Mercy is the desire to feel unusual empathy and compassion for those who are suffering or in desperate or temporary needs. This is the ability to bring comfort, support, and resources to alleviate the distress of the needy with uncanny delight.

A recommended procedure for developing this give would include:

- Identify persons with the gift of mercy that you admire.
- Dialogue with them about how they seem to know how to discern the needs of others that can be met if someone cared and got involved.
- Inquire about how they learned to discern the difference between the con artist, and the genuinely needy. Find the genuinely helpless and demonstrate how much you care.
- Look for the most difficult or unsightly circumstances that no one else cares about to cheerfully identify with and help through their situation.
- Ask your Bible class, church organization or activity if you could help them get involved in helping the needy in your community: have specific projects.
- Learn the art of how to help people become self-sustaining and to persuade others to help them.

Areas or type of service could include the following areas:

Home/Hospital/Institution Visitation, Transportation to Worship/Bible Study, or other transportation needs, Social Ministry Team, Support Group Leader, helping families or individuals going through disasters, or hospitalization, Seek out families of abandoned parents, prisoner's families, military, or bereaved needing care.

Which of these appeal to your interests: _____

Write out the desires of your heart of what you want to do for the Lord with this gift:

_____

_____

What are you going to begin doing this week to practice this gift?

_____

_____

Discernment

Symptoms and definitions:

Discernment is the special ability to know intuitively whether a certain behavior, teaching or character is from God, Satan, human error or human power. These persons have the ability to know in whom to trust.

A recommended procedure for developing this give would include:

- Gaining a comprehensive understanding of Proverbs, Ecclesiastes, and the commands of Scripture.
- Identify persons with the gift of discernment that you admire.
- Dialogue with them about how they seem to know how to discern the truth from error and the genuine from the untrustworthy.
- Ask other leaders about how they learned to

Areas or type of service could include the following areas:

Congregation Council, Long Range Planning Team, Social Ministry Team, Peer Counseling, Support Group Facilitator, selection of teachers, Committee for pastor-selections, or special speakers.

Which of these appeal to your interests: _____

Write out the desires of your heart of what you want to do for the Lord with this gift:

_____

_____

What are you going to begin doing this week to practice this gift?

_____

_____

Evangelism

Symptoms and definitions:

Evangelism is the special ability to quickly and clearly be able to express the salvation message in multiple situations with freedom and conviction that is convincing to the hearer.

A recommended procedure for developing this give would include:

- Gaining a comprehensive understanding of passages that deal with the concept of the salvation message and all the terminology used in the NT.
- Identify persons with the gift of evangelism that you admire.
- Dialogue with them about how they seem to know how to boldly and consistently share the gospel in many different kinds of situations.
- Ask other leaders about how they learned to evangelize; ask if they would take you to evangelize and critique your presentation.
- Find a partner to hold yourself (and them) accountable for weekly witnessing to the unsaved.

Areas or type of service could include the following areas:

Prospective Member Visitation, Evangelism Team, Advertising and Marketing, New Member Sponsor, Community Visitation, teaching evangelism to individuals or classes, Small Group leader.

Which of these appeal to your interests: _____

Write out the desires of your heart of what you want to do for the Lord with this gift:

_____

_____

What are you going to begin doing this week to practice this gift?

_____

_____

Exhortation or encouragement

Symptoms and definitions:

Exhortation is the ability to graciously confront, challenge and refocus believers on the biblical principles, examples and commands of Scripture. They have the ability to keep the week from faltering and the fainthearted believers from discouragement. They believe profoundly that God's way of living is the only fulfillment in this life.

A recommended procedure for developing this give would include:

- Gaining a comprehensive understanding of passages that deal with the commands, principles and examples in the Bible.
- By personally applying the commands to one's personal life and learning how to face life's situations regardless of one's emotions, then others will listen to you.
- Identify persons with the gift of exhortation that you admire.
- Dialogue with them about how they seem to know how to speak to the root issue in a person's life and the person appreciates their help.
- Be convinced that by learning the instructions in God's Word then deciding how to practice them one begins to grow spiritually.
- Learn how to help people become accountable for obedience.

Areas or type of service could include the following areas:

Mutual Ministry Team, Hospital/Home/Institution Visitation, Tele-care Ministry, Peer Counseling, Small Group Leader, ministry counselor, or

Which of these appeal to your interests: _____

Write out the desires of your heart of what you want to do for the Lord with the gift of exhortation or encouragement gift:

_____

_____

What are you going to begin doing this week to practice this gift?

_____

_____

Faith

Symptoms and definitions:

Faith is the special ability to never loose confidence in God's ability to intervene, meet impossible needs, fulfill His will in every circumstance and to never succumb to discouragement. This attitude must become contagious throughout the congregation as it is demonstrated, especially in seemingly impossible situations.

A recommended procedure for developing this give would include:

- Gaining a comprehensive understanding of passages that deal with the promises of God, discerning the will of God and the rewards of trusting His will in the NT.
- Identify persons with the gift of faith that you admire.
- Dialogue with them about how they seem to know what God's will is in many different kinds of situations and how they learned to trust God's ability.
- Ask other leaders about how they learned to have faith in their most discouraging situations.
- After prayer over situations, trust God for specific goals that He alone could accomplish. Begin with small goals encouraging others to trust God together with you for their fulfillment.
- Celebrate every answer to prayer to honor God and encourage others to trust Him more.
- Do not be afraid to dream of tasks that would honor His name, expand the gospel acceptance and meet the needs of His people

Areas or type of service could include the following areas:

Congregational President, Stewardship Team, Long Range Planning Team, Bible study leader

Which of these appeal to your interests: _____

Write out the desires of your heart of what you want to do for the Lord with this gift:

_____

_____

What are you going to begin doing this week to practice this gift?

_____

_____

Giving

Symptoms and definitions:

Giving is the unusual ability to sacrificially give beyond one's normal capacity (without going into debt) to meet the needs of others, though often creating a personal need or lack of resources. The spiritual ability to give is more than generosity, but also entails the lack of personal need for recognition, gratitude or even thankfulness. God is their recompense and reward. The important factor is that needs are met, not that credit is gained.

A recommended procedure for developing this give would include:

- Gaining a comprehensive understanding of passages that deal with the concept of giving and eternal rewards as used in the NT.
- Identify persons with the gift of giving that you admire.
- Dialogue with them about how they seem to know when to be generous, sacrificial and how they handle the giving up of things.
- Ask other leaders about how they learned to give beyond their means, and what principles guide their giving.
- Watch others and pray about how to be an encouragement to others without seeking glory to one's self for giving.
- Find a partner to hold yourself (and them) accountable for weekly giving generously.
- Begin to practice giving to others in secret.

Areas or type of service could include the following areas:

Capital Campaign Steering Team, Stewardship Team, Volunteer Coordination, Giving Personal Testimony, teach stewardship principles in classes.

Which of these appeal to your interests: _____

Write out the desires of your heart of what you want to do for the Lord with this gift:

_____

_____

What are you going to begin doing this week to practice this gift?

_____

_____

Helps, Serving

Symptoms and definitions:

The gifts of Helps and Serving are similar to each other and statistically they are the most common gift in the body of Christ. This gift enables the person to gladly work behind the scenes taking care of details to facilitate the work of God. It is the investing of time, talents, and resources for the ministry and serving individuals as well. The spiritual quality is evident when recognition and recompense are not needed or sought, rather God's grace and power brings sufficient motivation to continue sacrificing for the benefit of others.

A recommended procedure for developing this give would include:

- Gaining a comprehensive understanding of passages that deal with the concept of serving and eternal rewards in the NT.
- Identify persons with the gift of serving and helping that you admire. Recognize how these gifts have been a personal benefit to you.
- Dialogue with they see the tangible and practical tasks that need to be done and how they enjoy doing them.
- Ask other leaders about how they learned the value of helping and serving others.
- Find a partner to hold yourself (and them) accountable for weekly helping or serving in the ministry and individuals in your sphere of life.

Areas or type of service could include the following areas:

Computer Programmer/Data Entry, Building Maintenance/Upkeep Electrical/Masonry/Plumbing/Roofing Mechanical Repair/Maintenance Audio/Visual Operator and Repair Computer Maintenance, Web-Page Developer, P.A./Sound System Technician

Which of these appeal to your interests: _____

Write out the desires of your heart of what you want to do for the Lord with this gift:

_____

_____

What are you going to begin doing this week to practice this gift?

_____

_____

Leadership

Symptoms and definitions:

Leadership is the special ability to gain the confidence of others as their leader by their self-confidence, clarity of expression, conviction of purpose, vision and goals and the ability to engender a spirit of harmony, self-sacrifice and commitment to objectives that will bring glory and honor to God.

A recommended procedure for developing this give would include:

- Gaining a comprehensive understanding of passages that deal with the concept of biblical leadership in the NT, especially as distinct from secular leadership principles.
- Identify persons with the gift of leadership that you admire.
- Dialogue with them about how they seem to know how to fearlessly take leadership roles and responsibility.
- Ask other leaders about how they learned to how to lead under biblical principles of leadership.
- Find a partner to hold yourself (and them) accountable for taking responsibility for task completions.

Areas or type of service could include the following areas:

Sunday School Superintendent, Committee Chairperson (all types), Fellowship Activity Coordinator, Vacation Bible School Coordinator, Congregational President, Speaker: Special Events

Which of these appeal to your interests: _____

Write out the desires of your heart of what you want to do for the Lord with this gift:

_____

_____

What are you going to begin doing this week to practice this gift?

_____

_____

Pastoring

Symptoms and definitions:

Pastoring is the special ability to care enough about others to take responsibility for their spiritual maturity and ministry fulfillment. This is the divine ability to give guidance, teaching practical principles from God's Word and warn believers of dangerous habits, false teaching and positive guidance from His Word.

A recommended procedure for developing this give would include:

- Gaining a comprehensive understanding of passages that deal with the concepts of spiritual maturity, correct doctrine, all the commands, and biblical principles for Christian living in the NT.
- Identify persons with the gift of pastoring that you admire.
- Dialogue with them about how they desired to take responsibility and desire for overseeing the lives of others, and what motivates them in the ministry.
- Begin with a small Bible study, both for how to teach and how to care for everyone under your watch.
- Find a partner to hold yourself (and them) accountable for caring for others.

Areas or type of service could include the following areas:

Adult In-Home Bible Study Leader, New Member Sponsor, Young-Adult Counselor, Small Group Leader, lead an Adult or young people Bible Class, Telecare Ministry

Which of these appeal to your interests: _____

Write out the desires of your heart of what you want to do for the Lord with this gift:

_____

_____

What are you going to begin doing this week to practice this gift?

_____

_____

Teaching

Symptoms and definitions:

Teaching is the special ability to clearly explain the truths of God's Word and apply them effectively so that they become unforgettable and directly applicable to their lives. The power of the spiritual gift is evident in the ability to prepare and reflect for long hours for accuracy and personal application, then to teach with interaction for hours resulting in lives changed and deeper commitments to God's Word.

A recommended procedure for developing this give would include:

- Gaining a comprehensive understanding of the OT and NT, and how to interpret it accurately.
- Identify persons with the gift of teaching that you admire.
- Dialogue with them about how they seem to know how to gain their understanding of God's Word and how they sense the proper application of their findings.
- Ask other leaders about how they study, what tools they use, and what disciplines they practice daily in their study habits.
- Find a partner to hold yourself (and them) accountable for weekly studying God's Word in a systematic manner to master a portion of God's Word weekly.

Areas or type of service could include the following areas:

Adult Bible Class Teacher, Sunday School Teacher, Teen Bible Class Teacher, Vacation Bible School Teacher, Conference/Seminar Leader, a Small Group Bible Study teacher.

Which of these appeal to your interests: _____

Write out the desires of your heart of what you want to do for the Lord with this gift:

_____

_____

What are you going to begin doing this week to practice this gift?

_____

_____

Word of Wisdom (speaking gift)

Symptoms and definitions:

Word of wisdom is similar to exhortation, and teaching, with the ability to have the unusual ability to apply the Word of God in practical way to life's situations. The knowledge of the principles of God's Word are easily recalled for decision-making and life-application.

A recommended procedure for developing this give would include:

- Gaining a comprehensive understanding of passages that deal with the concepts of the will of God, principles, examples and insights into the mind of Christ in the NT.
- Identify persons with the gift of wisdom that you admire.
- Dialogue with them about how they seem to know which principles to apply in counseling and corrections to wayward believers.
- Ask other leaders about how they learned the principles of counseling and advice from God's Word.
- Find a partner to hold yourself (and them) accountable for weekly applying and conquering sin and temptation in one's personal life.

Areas or type of service could include the following areas:

Long Range Planning Team, Congregation Council Peer Counselor, Support Group Leader, Mutual Ministry and Accountability Team

Which of these appeal to your interests: _____

Write out the desires of your heart of what you want to do for the Lord with this gift:

_____

_____

What are you going to begin doing this week to practice this gift?

_____

_____

www.ingramcontent.com/pod-product-compliance
Lightning Source LLC
Chambersburg PA
CBHW080936040426
42443CB00015B/3430